# Invitation

**OneBook.**

# Invitation

## A TEN-WEEK BIBLE STUDY
with Brian D. Russell

Scripture quotations are taken from the HOLY BIBLE, TODAY'S NEW INTERNATIONAL VERSION˚ TNIV˚. Copyright © 2001, 2005 by Biblica www.biblica.com. All rights reserved worldwide.

Printed in the United States of America

Print ISBN: 978-1-62824-135-8
Mobi ISBN: 978-1-62824-136-5
ePub ISBN: 978-1-62824-137-2
uPDF ISBN: 978-1-62824-138-9

Library of Congress Control Number: 2014955588

*Cover Design by Nikabrik Design*
*Page design by PerfecType, Nashville, Tennessee*

SEEDBED PUBLISHING
Franklin, Tennessee
Seedbed.com
SOWING FOR A GREAT AWAKENING

With gratitude to the God who loves me and whose grace
has always proven itself sufficient.

# CONTENTS

# CONTENTS

CONTENTS

## Chapter Six

### God's Holy Vision for His Missional People          125

## Chapter Seven

### Israel's Life in the Land: The Potential and Pitfalls of Living as God's Missional People          149

## Chapter Eight

### The Prophets: Servants of Faithfulness and Proclaimers of God's Future          173

CONTENTS

## Chapter Nine
## Jesus, the Church, and God's Mission 197

## Chapter Ten
## Church and New Creation 225

# PUBLISHER'S FOREWORD: ONEBOOK BIBLE RESOURCES

Welcome to OneBook, the Bible study resource brought to you by Seedbed. In all of the history of the world, one book stands in a category of its own. Obviously, we read many books during the course of our lives but one book towers over them all. I'm referring, of course, to the Bible—the Word of God.

Unparalleled in truth and unmatched in wisdom, the Bible tells us the story of the world, from Creation to New Creation. It reveals the reality of God—Father, Son, and Holy Spirit—and teaches us what it means to be a human being, created in the image of God, broken by sin yet redeemed by grace and destined for a life of profound purpose and deep meaning.

As a result, the Bible is worthy of our highest attention and deepest devotion. To be sure, it is a complex book, actually made up of sixty-six books, written in three different languages, over the course of 1500 years across three continents by over forty authors. It is in the marvel of such complexity that we discover the miracle of its simplicity: from beginning to end, Genesis to Revelation, the Bible tells a single, unified story.

John Wesley once famously said:

> I am a spirit come from God, and returning to God: just hovering over the great gulf; till, a few moments hence, I am no more seen; I drop into an unchangeable eternity! I want to know one thing—the way to heaven; how to land safe on that happy shore. God himself has condescended to teach me the way. For this very end He came from heaven. He hath written it down in a book. O give me that book! At any price, give me the book of God! I have it: here is knowledge enough for me. Let me be a man of one book.[1]

We want to invite and inspire you to give yourself to a lifelong study of the Bible. We want you to become a person of OneBook. We are determined to help you read it for all it's worth, and to understand it and what it says about God's purposes for your life. This is not so much a book we seek to master as a book we seek to be mastered by.

We have carefully chosen teachers—men and women—who have given their lives to understanding Scripture and who in the process have stood under its teaching. We have searched for exemplars who love Jesus, who love the church, and who love people.

We are pleased to present to you an introductory study entitled, *Invitation*, with Dr. Brian Russell. This ten-week study includes a daily study guide and a weekly thirty-minute video teaching session.

*Invitation* can be engaged individually, however, it is recommended as a group study. As the title indicates, this study will work well for people who have never studied the Bible. Likewise, Dr. Russell's handling of the text will offer depth of insight to even the most learned Bible students.

**Brian Russell** is a seasoned teacher of Scripture. As a professor of biblical studies his expertise is in the Old Testament; however, he approaches Scripture with a decisively New Testament approach to the mission of the church. He has planted churches, pastored, and taught in local churches for decades. Brian is an ordained pastor, a husband, and a father. You will be delighted by the Word of God, drawn closer into relationship with Jesus Christ, and discipled in the ways of the Holy Spirit through his teaching.

# PREFACE

Several years ago in the springtime, my daughters and I took a trip to the beaches south of Cape Canaveral on the east coast of Florida. It was a beautiful day. The sky was blue. The air was cool. The sun's rays warmed our faces. The waves rolled gently onto the shoreline. The water was clear, but too cold for us Floridians. Only a few brave tourists from much colder climates were splashing about in the water. But it was a perfect day for a walk along the shoreline. My daughters and I picked up seashells, chased gulls, and watched a group of skates cruising just below the surface a few yards offshore.

As we walked north toward the jetty that marked the entrance into Port Canaveral, my daughters spied an unusual object about fifty yards ahead of us. They immediately ran to see what it was. As they drew near, they began jumping up and down and waving wildly for me to move faster. I walked a little quicker, still not sure what the object was. Finally, when I was almost on top of it, it came into focus. It was a discarded five-gallon blue paint bucket. The bucket had washed ashore and most of it lay buried beneath wet sand. It had been out to sea for some time as the several dozen attached barnacles attested. The barnacles were still alive and they flexed in and out of their shells.

This was a remarkable sight, but my daughters immediately noted the precarious nature of the situation for the barnacles. The sun would soon dry them up and already a large flock of gulls gathered a few yards out of the reach of my daughters. They squawked in delight as they anticipated a deliciously easy meal. My daughters looked at me and said in unison, "Dad, you have to save them!" Not wanting to disappoint my daughters, I attempted to dislodge the bucket from the sand. Unfortunately, the wet sand provided a firm lock on the bucket and I could not budge it. It would have taken a full-sized shovel to dig it out of the sand. Next, I attempted to pull the barnacles off of the bucket so that I could toss them back to the safety of the sea. I reached down and gripped one with my fingers. As I tried to pull it free from the bucket, I crushed the poor barnacle in my hand. The barnacles were so securely fastened to the bucket that it was impossible to remove them without simultaneously destroying them.

My rescue attempt was hopeless. I recognized that there was nothing that I could do. They were unable to release from the bucket. This was their natural defense against moving tides and predators. Yet the barnacles' predicament has haunted me. At some point in time, it had made perfect sense for them to attach to the bucket. But now the context had changed and they were in trouble. The story that they had begun to write was rapidly coming to an end *and* they were unable or unwilling to change. This would be their final act. If they could only let go and embrace a new future . . .

I distracted my daughters with the offer of pizza and ice cream and we left the barnacles and bucket behind. As I led my daughters back to our car, I pondered my own life's story. *Who am I? What are the limits to my existence? What is my purpose? What story shapes my life? Am I holding on to an old story line that requires updating or needs a new ending? Is there a better story or a more compelling story that will shape and unleash me to live fully in our world in times of joy or in times of sorrow; in times of plenty and in times of trouble?*

## The Bible as the True Story of Our Lives

I have found the Bible to be the most compelling story; I hope to guide you into a journey of discovering its riches. As my daughters and I walked through the sand away from the barnacles, I remembered my initial encounters with the Bible as a teenager. I was looking for meaning and answers. At a New Year's Eve gathering in 1984, my youth pastor, Steve, challenged our youth group to read through the New Testament in the coming year. I didn't immediately take up this charge but a few months into 1985 I was struggling personally and spiritually. I was unsure of who I was or who I was supposed to become. These were the typical struggles of adolescence, but it is often in such moments that we reach a crossroads in life.

I was in my bedroom reflecting and I remembered Steve's challenge to me. I looked over at my bookshelf and saw the Bible that I had received at my church in the fourth grade. I picked it up and turned to the book of Matthew. I prayed a simple prayer: "Lord, if you are real, reveal yourself to me. Amen."

I began the habit of reading the Bible that evening. Its richness and depth continues to astonish me with its good news about God and inspire me to live moment by moment as the person God created me to be.

One of the world's spiritual giants Aurelius Augustine (354–430 AD) became a follower of Jesus through a powerful encounter with the Scriptures. He shared his testimony in his classic work, *Confessions*. He had been learning about the Bible and the message of Jesus. At a pivotal moment in his life, Augustine was outside in his yard deeply longing for truth and praying in desperation to God. He shares this experience with us:

> So was I speaking and weeping in the most bitter contrition of my heart, when, lo! I heard from a neighboring house a voice, as of boy or girl, I know not, chanting, and oft repeating. 'Take up and read; Take up and read.' [*'Tolle, lege! Tolle, lege!'*] Instantly, my countenance altered, I began to think most intently whether children were wont in any kind of play to sing such words: nor could I remember ever to have heard the like. So checking the torrent of my tears, I arose; interpreting it to be no other than a command from God to open the book, and read the first chapter I should find.[2]

Augustine goes on to describe how a copy of Paul's Letter to the Romans from the New Testament was nearby. He picked it up and opened it to chapter 13. Paul's words gripped Augustine and transformed his life. The Bible's story became Augustine's story. He grew to serve as one of the church's great theologians and leaders. The Bible desires to become the narrative that shapes our lives as well.

The Bible tells a poignant and timeless story. It offers narratives, proverbs, songs, poems, prophecy, apocalyptic visions, instructional letters, law, directions for worship, and even genealogies. But at the end of the day, the Bible as a whole weaves all of these elements and genres together into a tapestry that guides us to live as the people whom God created us to be.

## The Invitation

Over the next ten weeks, we will explore the overarching story of the Bible as a means of inviting you to taste and experience the power of the Scriptures personally or, perhaps even better, in the company of others hungry for a fresh vision of life as God intended it to be. As you prepare to begin our study, my prayer for you is that the Scriptures will astonish you. Whether you have some previous experience of the Bible or none at all, open yourself up to its message and pray a simple prayer. This is one that I often use: "God, I am here ready to listen and receive all that you have for me. Astonish me with your Word. In Jesus' name, Amen."

# ACKNOWLEDGMENTS

*Invitation* emerges out of the last decade of my reflection and teaching of the Scriptures at Asbury Seminary and in various settings around the country. I am grateful for so many who have shaped my thinking, provided encouragement, and walked with me on the journey of faith.

The writing of *Invitation* has been a pleasure and a labor of love. I am grateful for J. D. Walt and Andrew Miller of Seedbed for the opportunity to take on this project and for their enthusiastic support each step of the way. Thank you, Ryan Staples, for capturing my live teaching for the video component. Equally I wish to thank Holly Jones and her team of editors for helpful suggestions that strengthened the manuscript and cleaned up my many errors.

Thank you to the hundreds of students at Asbury Theological Seminary who listened carefully to early versions of the content of *Invitation* and asked great questions that helped me to expand and further develop the presentation.

I am likewise grateful for the many passionate followers of Jesus at places as diverse as the Youth Ministry Institute, Vineyard Church, Family Bible Camp, International Mentoring Network, University of Georgia Wesley Foundation, and First United Methodist Winter Park, who kept asking for the book version of my presentation on the missional overview of Scripture. Here it finally is!

Thank you to my good friends Eric Currie, Bill Tillmann, Bob Tuttle, Steve Harper, Tarquin Adams, and Richard Kravetz who have been there during critical moments in my life to help me stand when I might have otherwise fallen.

Thank you to my parents, Dale and Midge Russell, who raised me well and have loved me extravagantly throughout my life.

I am deeply grateful for my daughters, Micaela and Katrina. The privilege of fatherhood has made me a better man, and I seek to live out the story of this book as a witness to God for you. May you grow up wise and deep as a testimony to the faithfulness of God.

Thank you to my step-children, Sarah, Pati, Nana, and Bebo, along with my step-grandchildren, Athena and Nicholas. You have been a blessing to me and offered many kindnesses.

And finally, *gracias para ti mi amor*, Astrid, for creating a life with me of new beginnings, beautiful days, and pure joy. Your unconditional love kept me grounded and created an environment for the words of *Invitation* to flow effortlessly during the hours I spent writing in our home. Life is beautiful with you.

# ABOUT THIS STUDY

Welcome to *Invitation: A Ten-Week Bible Study*. This fast-paced survey will acquaint you with the entire biblical story from Genesis to Revelation. The author and instructor Dr. Brian Russell has been teaching this dramatic narrative to seminary students and church members alike for many years. In that time he has come to understand the many various points of confusion and areas of questioning that most people have as they are first introduced to the Bible.

*Invitation* is ideal for beginners who are new to the faith and attempting to get their bearings as they consider the Bible for the first time. Likewise, many longtime church attenders will find *Invitation* a valuable tool to help them fill in some of the blank places in their understanding; enabling them to better see the totality of the biblical story line. Most especially persons who know and love the Scriptures will find it useful when joining with those less familiar with the Bible as they come alongside them in classes, mentoring, or discipling. All of which are essential for new believers as they grow in their faith.

Each chapter of *Invitation: A Ten-Week Bible Study* is formatted with several consistent components:

- **Daily readings.** There are five daily readings which should be read prior to your weekly group session. Each reading has a Core Truth at the start of the reading and two or three questions which will help prompt you in your subsequent group discussion.
- **Weekly video.** Each week has a thirty-minute video presented by Dr. Russell. This video should be viewed during the weekly group session.
- **Weekly group session outline.** This outline will guide your group time. Please note that the outline recommends that the group time be opened and closed with prayer. You may wish to invite in advance different persons to lead these prayers. Many persons are hesitant

at first to pray publically so those who are reluctant may appreciate having a bit of warning as well as time to hear other more experienced "pray-ers" model this activity for them.

- **Conversation.** The conversation portion of the weekly meeting is the time where the earlier readings and video content are considered in context with the discussion prompts in the session outline.

Overall there may be more discussion material proposed here than can be covered in the normal session time. In our experience, participants always feel better about having too much to share rather than not enough. Those participating in the discussion will bring their own questions and concerns to the time together as well. Don't feel frustrated if all of the discussion material cannot be addressed in each session.

Since the study will require ten full weeks, we suggest that an introductory week be scheduled in which the group gathers, receives their books, has refreshments, and gets to know each other a bit. Participants can the use the following week to begin their daily reading and be ready to view the video and participate in the discussion when they have their first group session.

Group sessions will require a maximum of ninety minutes total. Since Dr. Russell is thoroughly teaching the material via the DVD and in the written text, the group leader is serving more as a host and facilitator of the discussion. Thus the leader doesn't need to be a biblical authority. His or her most important role is to insure that all participants have an opportunity to share. This is especially true in an introductory class such as this where those less familiar with the Bible may feel intimidated by others with more knowledge of Scripture. At its best this class is intended for those seeking to make sense of the complex story line of the Bible for the first time. The facilitator should be especially sensitive to the least experienced student to make certain that the most basic questions are not skipped over or minimized by the rest of the group.

This study should be a marvelous time to receive a solid inaugural grounding in Scripture or an excellent refresher course for persons with a spotty or incongruent understanding of the Bible. We encourage each person to invite the Holy Spirit into their life and into their group time so that hearts and minds will be opened anew to hear God's voice as they study his Holy Word.

# Invitation

# The Biblical Story

L ife is a story. Each of our lives tells a story and intersects with the stories of others. All of our stories weave together into the complex tapestries that form the human story. God desires to shape and transform all of these tapestries into a beautiful grand tapestry that points the world to God's goodness and love. To serve this purpose, God speaks to us through Scripture. Followers of Jesus call their Scriptures "the Bible," which means "The Book." The Bible is God's gift to us. The Bible narrates a story. It is the story of God's plans and actions for humanity and all creation. It includes God's perspective on the world as God intended at creation, how it is today, and how it will be in the future.

Some people think of the Bible as an answer book. But this can be misleading if we expect the Bible to answer every conceivable question we may want to ask. I think of it more as a book of questions that God wants us to ask of ourselves. If we read and ponder the Bible carefully, it will ask us questions and shape us with its answers. Since the beginnings of the Christ-following movement, God's people have read the Old and New Testaments as sacred Scripture. The biblical story proclaims a counter-story to every other human story. It engages every human culture and works to realign those cultures with the will and purposes of God. It does this by intersecting with our stories at key points but then offering a crossroads to lead us into the new story that God desires to write through us. The question for us is this: *What story primarily shapes our life?* This is a question that we must continually reflect upon as we read the Bible. But first let's look briefly at the broad contours of God's story in the Bible. The rest of this introduction will provide a snapshot of the Bible's content and provide a broad outline of how this study will proceed.

The Bible contains the story of God's purposes for humanity and the world. It can be summarized in six movements: creation, the fall, Israel, Jesus the Messiah, the church, and the New Creation.

## Creation

The biblical story begins with God's creation of a very good world (Gen. 1–2). This is an important beginning. The world that we find ourselves in today is not the world as God originally intended. God's original creation is a place of wonder and goodness. It is not fractured by violence or any form of evil. Instead, God fashions a place of abundance, beauty, and justice. As God creates, he evaluates his handiwork as "very good" (Gen. 1:31). God fills this earth with plants and living creatures. God creates humanity as a community of women and men to serve as his hands, feet, and mouthpieces—his ambassadors to and stewards of creation. Remember this. God created us for his mission. The Bible emphasizes the importance of men and women in God's plans by declaring that God has crafted all humanity in the very image of God. The invisible Creator desires to manifest his character and plans through the lives of the human community. In the beginning, humanity lives in a garden of abundance and experiences harmonious relationships between humanity and God, between humanity and creation, and between women and men. This is Eden and life as God intended it.

## The Fall

But the biblical epic takes a pivotal turn in Genesis 3–11. In these chapters, humans choose their own way over God's. The Bible calls this sin. Sin exists because God allowed for its possibility. Authentic relationships require choices. God did not create robots when he made us. God desires humanity to live eternally in communion with him. This is the highest and best purpose for all people, but God did not compel the first humans to obey (nor does he compel us). In the stories of these chapters, humanity chooses to live outside the boundaries of God's purposes. This choice has profound implications. It fractures the created order and causes a breach in the harmony of creation. Humanity falls short as stewards of creation and in its role of embodying the invisible God to creation. These stories teach that humanity has lost its way. But God does not give up on his creation. Rather, God responds by reaching out to bring healing and reconciliation to creation. The bulk of the biblical story is the narrative of God's mission to redeem and restore a lost humanity and broken creation. God's goal is to make it "very good" again.

## Israel: The People of God

### Israel's Ancestors

The remainder of the biblical story narrates God's solution to problem of a lost humanity and fractured creation. In the rest of the Old Testament, God calls forth a new humanity (Israel) to serve as his special people and as agents of God's blessings to the nations. The story of Israel begins with Abram (later Abraham) in Genesis 12. God chooses to use a family to initiate his plan of salvation. God's mission will advance through Abram's descendants. He calls Abram and his wife, Sarai (later Sarah), out of the context and turmoil of Genesis 3–11 to be the first family of a new humanity through whom God will bless all nations (Gen. 12:3). He blesses them so that they can be a blessing to the world. This will be a pattern throughout the Bible's story. An encounter with God's graciousness is always a commission to God's mission. It will be through Abram and his descendants that God's mission of salvation will reach its climax.

The life, death, and resurrection of Jesus will serve as the fullest expression of God's mission that begins with Abram (see Matt. 1:1). But we are getting ahead of the story. God calls Abram and Sarai to migrate to a new promised land: Canaan. God gives Abram a new name: Abraham. God then gives Abraham and Sarai a promised son, Isaac, in their old age. God's blessings flow to Isaac who has two sons, Esau and Jacob. The mission of God moves forward through Jacob's side of the family. Jacob's twelve sons give the names to the twelve tribes who will soon become the nation of Israel. Late in life Jacob and his entire family migrate to Egypt during a time of famine.

## Deliverance from Egypt

Israel lives in Egypt initially as guests, but soon Egypt's pharaohs enslave God's people and thwart God's mission to bless the nations through Israel. This oppression sets the stage for God's fundamental actions of salvation in the Old Testament: God's dramatic deliverance of his people from slavery in Egypt, the establishment of covenant with his people at Sinai, and the return of his people to the Promised Land. God delivers his people from Egypt, the dominant superpower of the time, through a decisive demonstration of his power and ability to save. He does this as a means of revealing his name and glory to all the earth (Exod. 9:16). God shows himself to be incomparable to all other gods (Exod. 15:11) and the true king of all creation (Exod. 15:18).

## Covenant at Sinai

At Sinai (Exodus 19–Numbers 10:10)[3], God reminds and recalls Israel to the mission given to Abraham: God's people are to serve as a missional community that reflects his character in/to/for the nations and the world (Exod. 19:4–6). At Sinai, God invites his people into a special relationship that the ancient world called a covenant. In this covenant, God's people agree to live out God's ethic to the world. This ethic may be summarized as "Love God and love others." God pledges himself to his people as their unique deity. God's people will serve as his hands, feet, and mouthpieces in the world in the service of God's mission to bless the nations. The bulk of Exodus–Deuteronomy describes the way in which God's people are to live to embody his character in the worship of God and in their relationships with one another before the eyes of the nations. These books also warn God's people about the dangers of idolatry, injustice, and unfaithfulness to their fulfilling God's mission in the world.

## Promised Land, Kingship, Temple, and Exile

The remainder of the Old Testament's historical books (Joshua–Nehemiah) narrate the potential and pitfalls of living as God's missional people in the world. God settles Israel in the land originally promised to Abraham. These books recount times of blessing in which God's people are faithful to their covenantal commitments. High points include Joshua's generation in settling the land, the rise of David and his kingdom, Solomon's building of the temple in Jerusalem, the reforms of Hezekiah and Josiah, and the renewal of God's people in the days of

Ezra and Nehemiah. But much of these books tell of the unfaithfulness of God's people through their practices of idolatry and injustice. These practices ultimately cause the destruction of God's temple in Jerusalem and the exile of God's people to Babylon. This part of Israel's story serves as a warning to future generations of God's people. Faithfulness matters in God's mission to bless the nations. Idolatry and injustice remain potent forces that compete with God's desire for faithfulness.

### God's Prophets

What is the meaning of the unfaithfulness of God's people and how does God react to it? God's people are unable and often unwilling to live faithfully within his covenant. They turn away from their exclusive relationship with God by pursuing other gods and goddesses. They also practice injustice within the community and by mistreating outsiders. In response, God sends his prophets. The books of Judges through 2 Chronicles contain some stories and words of the prophets, but the prophetic books (Isaiah–Malachi) record the vast majority of the messages of the prophets.

The prophets serve primarily to call God's people to realign with their God-given mission of reflecting God's character in, to, and for the world. The prophets address God's people and demand them to return immediately to God's ways. The prophets call God's people back to the ethos and mission described for God's people in Genesis–Deuteronomy. But the prophets also point forward to a future work of God in which God will usher in a new age of salvation. The prophets foresee a time in which God will act decisively to advance his mission to bless the nations, redeem humanity, and heal all creation. This new age will be known as the kingdom of God. Much of the expectation centers on visions of a messiah or descendant of David who will rise up and once again serve as king of God's people. It is fitting that the Old Testament ends with the writings of the prophets, as they function as a natural bridge to the arrival of Jesus and his gospel of the kingdom.

## Jesus the Messiah

The New Testament opens with Jesus announcing the arrival of the kingdom of God. This is the beginning of the new age of salvation envisioned by the prophets. The New Testament continually references and alludes to the Old

Testament to make it clear that God's new work in Jesus is an extension and fulfillment of the Old Testament. Jesus proclaims, teaches, and embodies the kingdom through his words and deeds. Jesus' preaching and actions emphasize the kingdom's openness to the marginalized among God's people and even to foreigners. Jesus dies a sacrificial death by crucifixion for the sins, injustices, and suffering of the world. He dies as Israel's messiah who lays down his life willingly for the sake of others. The cross is God's answer to the brokenness, shame, and lostness of humanity and all creation. God vindicates Jesus' life and death by raising him from the dead on the third day. Jesus' resurrection announces God's victory and ushers in the age of the church in anticipation of New Creation.

## The Church

Following his resurrection, Jesus sends his followers into the world to live as God's missional community that reflects God's character in, to, for the nations. The church goes out in the power of the Holy Spirit. God's people serve as witnesses and clues to the reality of the kingdom of God. They proclaim the good news of God's salvation and healing. The New Testament teaches the earliest Christians how to live as God's people with the goal of extending God's salvation to the world through the testimony of their words and lives. Each book offers reflection and instruction for living as God's holy and missional people. The dominant ethic of the early church was a commitment to reaching others. Each church in the fledgling Christ-following movement was a kingdom outpost surrounded on all sides by competing religions and ideologies.

The apostle Paul's writings dominate the second half of the New Testament following the four Gospels and Acts. Paul is a central actor in the book of Acts. He epitomizes the "go to" ethos of the New Testament. Through the faithfulness of Paul and his companions, God propels the gospel across much of the Roman Empire. Paul and his associates start new churches and move on to the next place where the true God is not yet known. The writings of the New Testament take seriously the challenges of living as God's people in a world that does not share or encourage the values of the gospel. Reading these books helps us today to understand and embody the good news of Jesus for the watching world.

## The New Creation

The New Testament ends with a vision of a secure future in God's New Creation. All creation returns to relational wholeness and goodness. The New Testament does not lay out a precise road map or time line to this future. The New Testament's visions of the future are not couched in some code that we can decipher nor are they intended to give us a play-by-play description. They exist to encourage believers to remain faithful witnesses in the present in the full confidence that God's desired future is secure and will be wonderful. Most of the New Testament books address the future in some way, but God's good future dominates the overall vision of Revelation, the final book of the Bible. Just as the first two chapters of Genesis begin the Bible with a description of a very good creation, the final two chapters of Revelation bring the biblical story to a conclusion by describing the New Creation as a New Heaven and New Earth. The abundance, goodness, peace, and justice of the original creation returns and God is enthroned and recognized as Lord of Creation while dwelling forever with God's people. Creation is as God intended it and humanity serves forever as God's missional community that reflects God's glory.

This is the story that we will explore in greater detail. This is the story that God desires for us to use as an authoritative guide to living the life of God's dreams. This is the story that will invite us to live as the people whom God has created us to be. We will now tell this story in more detail beginning with Jesus' proclamation of the kingdom.

## CHAPTER ONE

# Realigning with God—
# Jesus Proclaims the
# Kingdom

We start our journey through Scripture at the beginning of Jesus' ministry. Jesus' initial act is to announce the arrival of God's kingdom into the world. Jesus proclaims the good news that God's future age of salvation is now present and available to all. Jesus calls all who hear his message to realign their lives continually with values and ethic of the kingdom. In response to the arrival of God's kingdom, Jesus creates a new community that exists to spread the good news of the kingdom to the world by living as the people whom God created men and women to be.

# DAY 1

# Announcing a Kingdom

### Read Matthew 4:17

*From that time on Jesus began to preach, "Repent, for the kingdom of heaven has come near."—Matthew 4:17*

> **Core Truth:** Jesus calls all who hear him to realign themselves with the values and mission of God's age of salvation.

Jesus does not come to start a new religion; Jesus comes to unleash a kingdom. Jesus begins his public ministry by proclaiming boldly and audaciously the kingdom of God in Matthew 4:17.[4] Jesus the Son of God begins his ministry with a single sentence! Yet his words are thick with meaning. But it is a message embedded in the language and culture of the first century AD. We will need to unpack it. When we do, we will discover a profound word for the twenty-first century. Jesus' core message will then serve as a jumping-off point into the rest of the biblical story.

## Announcing God's Kingdom

Jesus' message contains two elements: 1) an exhortation to repent, and 2) the announcement of the arrival of God's kingdom as the reason for the repentance.

God's people in the first century longed for God to act to bring human history to a climax and to pour out God's saving power into the world. They considered the present world to be the age of evil. In the evil age, God's people were under the oppressive rule of the Roman Empire. Rome elevated its suffocating claims of power over all others. God's people suffered and languished. In addition to oppression, they faced similar issues to the ones we face today: economic uncertainty, lack of personal security, fears for their children's future, and political and societal upheaval. Yet in all of this, God's people waited for their God to act as he had in their Old Testament Scriptures when he delivered their ancestors from slavery in Egypt and raised up inspired leaders such as King David. Yes, God was still present, but they longed for a new day of salvation when God would make all things right and good again.

God's people called this future age the "kingdom of God" or "kingdom of heaven." Kingdom language implies that God is the true King over all the world. In the kingdom, God's people would enjoy peace, justice, mercy, kindness, forgiveness, and joy. So when Jesus opens his public ministry with kingdom language, he is tapping into the deepest longings of his audience and declaring that God's new era of abundance has arrived. Kingdom talk gained the attention of those who heard him speak. As we read through the Bible, we will talk about the gospel. In essence, the gospel is the good news about the arrival of God's kingdom through Jesus. There is no gospel without the good news of the kingdom.

When we talk about finding our place in the biblical story, we are talking about becoming persons that embody and proclaim the good news of the kingdom today. The Bible invites us to live as ambassadors of God's abundance and voices of hope for a world that desperately needs it. In the Lord's Prayer (see Matt. 6:9–13), Jesus teaches us to pray for the kingdom to manifest itself so that God's will is done equally on earth as it is in heaven. The sign of the kingdom is the will of God manifesting on earth. Wherever and whenever God's will is done, there is the kingdom. This is what Jesus' life will model.

## Realigning with God's Kingdom

How then do we respond to Jesus' announcement of the kingdom? Jesus frames our response with a single word, "Repent!" To repent is to make a radical reversal in life and realign with God. To repent or realign is a dynamic term that is more than a one-time event. Of course, there must be an initial turning to God, but the language of Matthew 4:17 indicates that repentance is a crisis moment *and* an ongoing way of life. We could more accurately capture Jesus' message by translating 4:17 "Repent continually" or "Be repenting continually." Jesus' words invite us to make sure that our lives are in alignment with God's character. This is a process that occurs moment by moment. Jesus calls us today to realign continually with the good news of the kingdom.

## Jesus' Audience

When Jesus announces the kingdom, he is addressing both deeply committed religious people as well as outsiders to the religion of Judaism such as Romans and Greeks and persons marginalized by its adherents including women, lepers, and the poor. By stressing the necessity of ongoing realignment, Jesus is able to direct a clear word that touches his audience whether they are an insider or an outsider to the ways of God. It's the same message. Jesus calls the person hearing the good news of the kingdom for the first time to align. Likewise, Jesus challenges the men and women who have previously aligned with his movement to realign.

Of course, realigning involves turning away from obvious evils and sins, but it also involves an ongoing assessment and shifting to better serve the mission of God in the world. As we read the Scriptures, we will hear them calling us to realign with God and become the people whom God created us to be. This is the message of the kingdom.

## Questions for Reflection

What about Jesus' initial words do you find interesting or inspiring?

_____

_____

What would it look like for you to realign with God today?

_____

_____

# DAY 2

# Missional Community

### Read Matthew 4:18–22

*As Jesus was walking beside the Sea of Galilee, he saw two brothers, Simon called Peter and his brother Andrew. They were casting a net into the lake, for they were fishermen. "Come, follow me," Jesus said, "and I will send you out to fish for people." At once they left their nets and followed him. Going on from there, he saw two other brothers, James son of Zebedee and his brother John. They were in a boat with their father Zebedee, preparing their nets. Jesus called them, and immediately they left the boat and their father and followed him.—Matthew 4:18–22*

> **Core Truth:** Following Jesus involves living as part of a community that guides and points others to God.

Jesus began his ministry by announcing God's kingdom and calling his audience to realign with it. What does it look like to realign with God?

Jesus begins to answer this in Matthew 4:18–22 by creating a new community that will embody the kingdom's values. This new community begins with two sets of brothers: Simon Peter and Andrew, and James and John, the sons of Zebedee. It is important for us to understand and see that the value and importance of community is embedded in the DNA of God's kingdom. We were created for community. Following Jesus involves being part of the new humanity that lives for God's kingdom.

## A Community for the World

Jesus' new community will embody the kingdom in the world, to the world, and for the world. Too often we can equate spirituality and religion with

15

separation from the surrounding world. Monks move away from society to live in monasteries. Priests and shamans wear distinctive clothing to mark their separation from the rest of humanity. Even ordinary Christians spend time away on retreats from the world. Jesus' new community will be different.

The community of Jesus exists not as an escape from the world but rather as an outpost for the kingdom of God. It is in the community of Jesus' followers where the kingdom of God is made manifest. Jesus' new community lives in anticipation of the coming day of abundance where all creation will bear witness to the justice, peace, joy, and love found in God. Until that day, Jesus' disciples serve as clues to the wider world of the good news of God's future.

## Communal Not Individualistic

There is a temptation in the spirituality of our world to focus solely on the individual. Christians sometimes talk about the need to have a personal relationship with Jesus. There is truth in this as each of us must answer Jesus' call to follow him. But notice that from the beginning of Jesus' ministry, he called two sets of brothers rather than merely solitary persons. There was never a moment when there was only Jesus and a single follower. He called brothers in part to signify that following Jesus means joining and participating in a new community. If Jesus were in our modern context, he would likely have called brothers and sisters or maybe even sisters. But the ancient world was male-driven and dominated, so a band of men was the only option to speak meaningfully to the culture of the ancient world. Moreover, Jesus' new community would eventually include twelve male disciples. This number was symbolic and meaningful for the Jews of Jesus' day because ancient Israel had been organized around twelve tribes that each traced their ancestry back to the twelve sons of Jacob/Israel (see chapter 4).

The implications of the necessity of community are vast. The fundamental truth is that we need each other in our journey of becoming all that God desires for us to be. Yes, each of us must exercise personal faith, but true faith manifests itself in relationships with others.

Those of us seeped in American mythology tend to amplify the hero over the collective. We tend to read the Bible as instructions for us as individuals. As we journey through the biblical narrative together, a key learning will be the *communal* nature of what it means to be a Christian as well as a human. God originally created humans for community. Part of our brokenness involves the fracturing of our relational lives. Jesus calls men and women to a new community. We genuinely need one another. We misread the Bible whenever we forget that Scripture speaks to us as people in community more than it addresses us merely as individuals. Each of us has a part to play. But we are part of a team.

## Missional Community as Clues to the Kingdom

God's people on mission serve corporately as clues to the reality of the kingdom. In the New Testament book of Philippians, Paul uses a powerful metaphor to describe how a missional community manifests the kingdom in the world, to the world, and for the world. In Philippians 2:15, he describes how God's people shine forth like stars. This is a rich image. Imagine the stars on the darkest of nights when you are far from the lights of any city. How do they appear? They leap off the fabric of the sky and radiate brightly. For millennia, humans have used the stars for guidance and to tell stories. Sailors have navigated their vessels by way of the stars. Storytellers have found pictures outlined by groupings of stars in order to narrate memorable tales. When Paul talks about shining like stars, he is reminding the Philippian Christians that their words and actions tell a story. Individual followers of Jesus serve as clues to the kingdom of God. The beauty of community is the possibility for enough clues to group together to point to the deepest truths about God's love and desire to bless the world.

## Questions for Reflection

How is your current understanding of the church challenged or stretched by the biblical emphasis on community?

_____

_____


Who currently walks with you in your journey with God into the world on mission? Who needs to join you?

_____

_____

# DAY 3

# The Mission and the Kingdom

Read Matthew 4:19

*"Come, follow me," Jesus said, "and I will send you
out to fish for people."—Matthew 4:19*

> **Core Truth:** The call to follow Jesus is a commission to serve as God's agents of blessing for the world.

When Jesus calls his first followers into his new community, he immediately initiates them into his mission. He calls them from their vocation of fishing to become part of a movement that will multiply itself by extending God's blessings to others. Notice the words that Jesus uses to call his initial disciples: "'Come, follow me,' Jesus said, 'and I will send you out to fish for people'" (Matt. 4:19). This text is vital for understanding what it means to be part of God's people. God's mission is central to the meaning of true spirituality. God's people are a community that exists for a purpose greater than itself. God's people are a missional community whose vocation is to share the good news of God's kingdom with the world.

## Mission as Central to Following Jesus

Much of Christianity today has lost its connection to God's mission. We are more likely to hear about following Jesus as a means of going to heaven than we are to hear about following Jesus into the world to extend God's blessings to others. If we want to recapture the original power of the Christ-following movement, we must reconnect spirituality and mission. We are blessed to be a blessing to others.

Following Jesus is a commission to mission. There is no waiting period before a disciple becomes a maker of disciples. It is significant to recognize that as soon as the brothers answer Jesus' call, they are now part of Jesus' mission.

## From Believing to Following

Words matter. We often hear more about "believing in Jesus" than "following Jesus." The New Testament does emphasize the necessity of faith and belief. Jesus does not use the phrase "follow me" to deny the importance of belief, but rather to make explicit its connection to life in the world. Jesus calls his followers to put their beliefs into immediate practice by living them out and embodying the deepest truths of the kingdom as a witness to the world.

Jesus' words, "follow me," also imply movement. Following Jesus is not an abstract intellectual pursuit. It is not detached from the world. It involves a moment-by-moment relationship with Jesus. Jesus models movement in the way he lived. As we read the Gospels, we will discover that Jesus moves from place to place and manifests the power and good news of the kingdom wherever he goes. Jesus teaches his disciples about God's mission by engaging them in his mission. Mission is about multiplying God's blessings to others. Jesus' mission includes shaping and forming new followers into people who can bless others while extending the kingdom to persons yet to experience it. Missiologist and thinker Alex McManus has often said, "The gospel comes to us on its way to someone else." This is the way of Jesus. As we hear Jesus' call to realign with the kingdom, we must hear this as an exhortation to God's mission in the world.

## Relevant Language

Notice the language Jesus uses to call his first disciples. His choice of words is illuminating. He engages his initial followers with words that are easily understood in their context. He speaks in words and metaphors from the lives of his listeners. Jesus' first followers are all fishermen. This is their livelihood and what they know best. He uses words that connect directly with their lives. Jesus calls fishermen to become a new type of fisherman: ones who fish for people. This is Jesus' way of translating the message of mission into the common language of his first followers. This is a crucial principle for us today as well. If we want to reach others with the good news of the kingdom, we need to learn enough about those whom we are seeking to serve so that we can use their language rather than insisting that they adopt our language. The implication of Jesus calling fishermen to become fishers of people is that if Jesus were calling, say, accountants or construction workers, he would use different words.

As we think about what it means to follow Jesus today, it is vital for us to recognize the centrality of mission. Jesus calls us so that we can be an extension of his mission. He invites us into relationship so that he can send us out to invite others. He blesses us so that we can bless others. When we follow Jesus, we function as Jesus' hands, feet, and mouthpieces in the world. We are clues that point to him.

## Questions for Reflection

How does Jesus' call to mission cause you to realign your understanding of the meaning of a spiritual life?

_____

_____

Who are the people in your life that God desires for you to serve and bless as God has blessed you?

_____

_____

# DAY 4

# A Holy Missional Community

### Read Matthew 4:18–22

*As Jesus was walking beside the Sea of Galilee, he saw two brothers, Simon called Peter and his brother Andrew. They were casting a net into the lake, for they were fishermen. "Come, follow me," Jesus said, "and I will send you out to fish for people." At once they left their nets and followed him. Going on from there, he saw two other brothers, James son of Zebedee and his brother John. They were in a boat with their father Zebedee, preparing their nets. Jesus called them, and immediately they left the boat and their father and followed him.—Matthew 4:18-22*

---

**Core Truth:** Jesus' followers reflect the character of God and the values of God's kingdom in their daily lives as they embody his mission.

---

Jesus calls disciples to follow him into the world and serve as a missional community. Central to this mission is the ethic or way of life that God's people live out. God's people are to reflect and embody the values of the kingdom in their lives together as Jesus' disciples and in their interactions with the wider world. God desires to do a transforming work in our lives so that we can be shaped into the people whom God created us to be.

## Mission and Holiness

We've already learned that the call to follow Jesus is a commission to mission. Following Jesus also involves serving as models of Jesus' way of life to the world. God desires that our lives manifest the values we hold and the mission we proclaim. Following Jesus involves learning both God's mission and the habits of life that show others the goodness and love of God. The Scriptures call this holiness. Holiness is a characteristic of God and one that he desires to be present in and modeled by his people. At its heart, holiness is love. If love is absent, God's mission is not advanced.

When Jesus says, "Follow me," he is calling his disciples to observe and imitate him. He desires to instruct and form in them habits of holy love. When we read the Gospels, the stories about Jesus serve to teach us how to live. They are not merely reports about the past. Following Jesus is about walking moment by moment with mindfulness. We follow Jesus so that we begin to live and act in ways than align with his life. The holiness that Jesus teaches is a missional holiness. Jesus' disciples don't become holy so that they can go on mission; they learn the necessity and way of holiness by engaging in mission.

## Missional Holiness as Light in the World

The holiness that Jesus teaches is not a flight from or separation from the world. Jesus' mission is to engage the world with the good news of the kingdom. Jesus understands that the kingdom is more dangerous to the world than the world is dangerous to the kingdom. Jesus engages the world in the confidence that his light will illuminate the darkness and spark new life and light in others. He is not worried about having his light snuffed out by the world.

Jesus' disciples model and reflect God's character as the means of bearing the light and blessings of God into even the darkest places on earth. When we read the Gospels, we encounter Jesus touching diseased persons without fear of contamination and driving out demons without fear of the power of evil. Jesus calls all of his disciples to ongoing and continual transformation as the essential means of carrying out his mission. The goal of transformation is the fulfillment and embodiment of the character of God in/to/for the world. Thus, holiness is a necessity to life on mission in the world.

When my youngest daughter, Katrina, entered kindergarten, some of my more religious friends disapproved of the decision to send her to public school. I was not worried about this. She was raised with the values of Jesus. Every day before school, I always prayed this prayer with her: "Live by faith, be known by love, and serve as a voice of hope for others. Amen." About two months into the school year, her teacher invited me to a conference to talk about Katrina's progress. The teacher's first words to me were this: "Mr. Russell, I want you to know that Katrina is a voice of hope in my classroom." My jaw dropped, but I should not have been surprised. This is how it's supposed to be. The message of the kingdom is more powerful than any danger lurking in the world.

## Mission, Holiness, and Community

Jesus' holiness is both individual and corporate. In Matthew 4:18–22, Jesus calls brothers into a community, but ultimately each one has to answer Jesus' call as an individual. In the Western world, we tend to focus on our individual walk with God apart from any communal commitment. We compartmentalize our religious or spiritual commitments apart from our work lives or interactions with others. But note that Jesus emphasizes the communal aspect. We are not called to solitary lives of holiness. Jesus' call to "follow" him as part of a missional community is a crucial step in becoming a disciple.

Holiness manifests itself most clearly and missionally in our relationships with others. It matters how we interact with other followers of Christ. It matters how we engage persons outside the circle of Christ-followers.

## Questions for Reflection

What kind of person do you hear Jesus calling you to become?

_____

_____

How would you need to change if you were to follow the way of Jesus?

_____

_____

How would your community need to change in order to prioritize mission and holy living?

_____

_____

# DAY 5

# God's GPS for Living

Read Psalm 119:105

*Your word is a lamp to my feet and a light for my path.*
*—Psalm 119:105*

---

**Core Truth:** Mission, community, and holiness are three core themes that serve to guide us through the Bible as God's GPS: Global Mission, Persons in Community, and Spirit-Transformed (holiness).

---

Jesus calls those of us living today to respond to the good news of the kingdom by realigning continually to his words and life as we find them in Scripture. In fact, Jesus' call to realign invites us to go back to the beginning of the Bible and read it from Genesis to Revelation as a journey of realignment.

## Reading Scripture as a Journey

What does the journey of realignment entail? What sort of life do the Scriptures imagine for us? How do we read them in a way that allows the scriptural story to transform rather than to merely inform? Life is a journey and the Bible is our authoritative guide to living as the people whom God created us to be. So the questions become: How do we get to where God wants us to be? What does the life of God's dreams for us look like?

In the modern world, when we take a journey, we have tools to help get us there. We can use maps. Many of us also use GPS navigational technology. GPS technology depends on the use of a series of satellites orbiting earth. As long as the traveler is able to triangulate his position with three available satellites, GPS systems are able to guide him to his final destination. They lead us by locating our position and continually realigning our movement so that we make it safely to the desired location. Airlines and ocean freighters use the technology as well. Remarkably, while en route, planes and ships using GPS are at any given moment slightly off course. But the GPS continually recalculates the position and the vessels are able to realign so that they end up safely where they are intending to go. Even in our cars, if we miss a turn or move in an unexpected way, our GPS recalculates our position and makes adjustments to our route in order to find the next best way to arrive at where we are going.

The Bible is the map to the life of God's dreams for us. But how do we figure out how to use it? Wouldn't it be great if there were a GPS for reading the Bible? We've already described the Bible as God's story. It is a story that seeks to shape us to live as God's people. Jesus' announcement of the kingdom is nothing more and nothing less than a reaffirmation of this intention. When we talk about a continual realigning of our lives with the values and ethics of the kingdom, we are talking about tapping into the navigational system that God has given us in the Bible.

## GPS for the Bible

We need a GPS system because God's story is about advancing the gospel. Jesus creates a movement. The gospel is always moving to bless those who do not yet know God. As Jesus' followers, Jesus calls us to follow him into the world (see Matt. 16:24; 28:18–20). Since we are moving, just like an airliner or ship with GPS, we will need to make ongoing realignments in order to stay on track to where Jesus is leading us.

Jesus' initial proclamation of the gospel and calling of his first followers serves as a model and paradigm of this navigational system. In announcing God's kingdom and calling disciples, Jesus creates a missional community that reflects and embodies the values and ethics of God's kingdom in the world, to the world, and for the world. Notice the three key themes present in Jesus' initial action: mission, community, and holiness. This triad of themes serves as the three points of God's GPS for reading Scripture. We can remember them through the use of an acronym:

G = God's mission (mission)
P = Persons in community (community)
S = Spirit-transformed (holiness)

As we move through the Scriptures, we will use these three themes to help us illuminate the message of the Bible and allow it to shape us as Jesus' disciples in, to, and for our world. Our spirituality is for the world; our community is for the world; and our mission is for the world. We will use GPS as a guiding light to see if it helps us to grow in God's grace and truth. We are not going to insist that every single text in the Bible speak to all three themes of GPS, but we will discover that most texts will engage at least one of these themes.

We also want to remember that we are reading the Bible together with others who may or may not consider themselves Jesus' followers. Just as Jesus proclaimed the kingdom without discriminating between insiders and outsiders to the kingdom, we must follow his example and listen to the Bible as a whole as an address to humanity. Those who are already seeking to listen to and walk with God need to hear the Scriptures as a continual call to realign with its message. Those who are on the boundaries of faith and exploring Jesus' message need to hear the Bible as an open invitation to align with Jesus for the first time. Jesus' message of realignment is open to all. We can use GPS as followers of Jesus desiring to grow in faith or as seekers of Jesus pondering making a commitment. In both cases, the Bible will call us to a deeper place as we align with Jesus and his kingdom.

Here are some questions that we will use to help us in our journey through the Scriptures:

## Global Mission

*Followers*: How does this text shape our understanding of God's mission in the world? How do we need to change to embody this mission for the world around us?

*Seekers*: What sort of world is this text inviting me to spend my life working to create? What would my life look like if I joined this mission?

## Persons in Community

*Followers*: How does this text envision the corporate life of God's people? How do God's people need to change in order to embody the portrait of community assumed by this text?

*Seekers*: What type of community is this text inviting me to explore? How is this text inviting me to participate in a community that exists for something greater than my own wants and desires?

### Spirit-Transformed

*Followers*: What sort of person do I need to become in order to live out this text? How do God's people need to change in order to more profoundly reflect the character of God?

*Seekers*: What type of lifestyle/character is this text inviting me to embody? How would my life be enriched by aligning my character with the vision of this text?

## Questions for Reflection

Describe your current understanding of the themes of mission, community, and holiness (GPS).

_____

_____

In what ways do you need to grow in mission, community, and holiness to become the person God created you to be?

_____

_____

# Realigning with God—
# Jesus Proclaims the Kingdom

## CORE TRUTHS

1. Jesus calls all who hear him to realign themselves with the values and mission of God's age of salvation.
2. Following Jesus involves living as part of a community that guides and points others to God.
3. The call to follow Jesus is a commission to serve as God's agents of blessing for the world.
4. Jesus' followers reflect the character of God and the values of God's kingdom in their daily lives as they embody his mission.
5. Mission, community, and holiness are three core themes that serve to guide us through the Bible as God's GPS: Global Mission, Persons in Community, and Spirit-Transformed (holiness).

## OPEN SESSION WITH PRAYER

Briefly introduce yourself and give each member of the group an opportunity to introduce themselves using these two questions: About what would the person who knows you best say that you are most passionate? Why are you interested in studying the Bible?

## DEBRIEF THE READING FOR THE WEEK (15 MINUTES)

- What were your key takeaways from this week's reading?
- What aspects of the reading did you find confusing?
- What is the kingdom of God?

- What does it mean to "repent" or "realign"?
- What are the themes for the Bible's GPS?

## WATCH VIDEO (30 MINUTES)

## CONVERSATION (15 MINUTES)

- What aspects of the message resonated with you most deeply?
- What questions did Brian's talk raise for you?
- How does Jesus' message of the kingdom challenge the realities of our present world?
- What does it mean for you to realign or repent today?
- Who is your mission?
- Who is the community with whom you will do life?
- What kind of person does Jesus' kingdom desire you to become?
- Who in your life needs to join us in our journey through the Scriptures?

## CLOSING PRAYER

## CHAPTER TWO

# Creation and the Mission of God

The beginning of the Bible narrates God's creation of a very good world. The Bible begins with a portrait of the world and life as God originally intended it. The story of creation introduces us to a God who creates a beautiful and wondrous world and crafts men and women to serve as his hands, feet, and mouthpieces of his goodness. God also orders his world to move from work to rest.

# DAY 1

# God Creates the Heavens and the Earth

### Read Genesis 1:1–2

*In the beginning God created the heavens and the earth. Now the earth was formless and empty, darkness was over the surface of the deep, and the Spirit of God was hovering over the waters.—Genesis 1:1–2*

---

**Core Truth:** Creation stories teach us about God, the world, and ourselves.

---

To understand who God is, who we are, and what the world is supposed to become, we must begin at the beginning. The book of Genesis opens with two narratives that describe creation as God intended it. The goal of the creation stories in Genesis is to introduce us to the only God who is truly worthy of our worship, service, and our lives and to show us the profound people whom God created us to be.

## The Challenge of Reading the Creation Stories in the Twenty-First Century

The opening chapters of Genesis present challenges for people living in the modern world. We grow accustomed to modern explanations of origins such as the Big Bang theory. Physicists tell us that the universe is almost fourteen billion years old. Nuclear scientists work with subatomic particles. In comparison, the Bible's story of beginnings is radically different. Genesis does not use modern scientific language. It uses language and imagery that made sense to ancient people. If we expect to find modern science in Genesis, we will be disappointed. But if we read and listen to Genesis as a means of realigning with God, Genesis will astonish us with its profound and deep truth.

Many of us wonder how the biblical accounts of creation match up with modern science. Often we reduce studies of Genesis 1–2 to a debate over creation in a single week against modern explanations such as the Big Bang or theories of evolutionary biology. Such questions are interesting, but the conversation that Genesis 1–2 desires to have with us is not primarily a scientific one. It is a theological and anthropological one. Genesis wants to ask us questions as much as it wants to answer our questions. Critical to understanding the Bible's creation narratives is the need to recognize that Israel's creation accounts do not exist in isolation. Israel's neighbors all had their own creation stories. These stories tried to make sense of the world and explain the relationship between humanity and the divine. Israel's neighbors worshiped many gods and goddesses. Israel's neighbors also had a vastly different understanding of the role and value of the average person. Creation stories served to shape the foundational beliefs of ancient people about the nature of God, themselves, and the world.

## Introducing God in a World of Many "Gods"

Genesis opens with a short sentence: "In the beginning God created the heavens and the earth" (1:1). The opening line declares that all creation is the handiwork of God. It introduces us to the key actor in the biblical story: God.

Who is God? This may not seem like an important question. We all know who God is, right? Yet this question cuts to the heart of what Genesis wants us to explore. In the ancient world, polytheism (the belief and worship of many gods and goddesses) was the norm. Every nation and tribe understood the divine within the framework of polytheism. To say the word "god" would only generate the question, "Which one?" Even in our twenty-first century context, "Who is God?" remains a vital question. God is a word that is used almost universally, but everyone has his or her own understanding of its meaning. As we read the Bible together, it is critical to allow the Scriptures to teach us about God rather than importing our own assumptions.

## What's in a Name? LORD Versus God

Notice that Genesis 1:1 uses the word "God." It is one of the two most common ways that the Old Testament talks about God. The other is "LORD." Of the two, LORD is God's personal name. LORD is the way that the ancient Israelites verbalized God's personal name, "Yahweh." Since the Bible is Yahweh's story, we might have expected Genesis 1:1 to begin, "In the beginning the LORD created the heavens and earth" rather than with the more generic name "God." But it doesn't. What difference does this make?

By beginning with the more generic term *God*, Genesis signals that all that the Bible expects of its readers is an openness to the reality of god or gods. The word translated "God" in 1:1 is the Hebrew word *Elohim*. Elohim is a plural noun and in a different context it could be translated "gods." In the Old Testament, when God's people write the word "Elohim," they of course mean God. Their use of a plural is their way of emphasizing the authority, distinctiveness, and power of their God the LORD over the gods of their neighbors. In Genesis 1:1–2:3, we will find that Elohim occurs thirty times. Elohim is the sole Creator. This claim is unmistakable. The exclusive and persistent use of Elohim makes it clear that Genesis desires for its readers to ask these questions: Who is Elohim? What is the name of this God?

If Genesis 1:1 had simply declared Yahweh (LORD) to be the Creator, it would have been a conversation stopper. Of course, the author of Genesis desires to declare and lift up the LORD as the Creator God, but he also wants to engage the world with this truth in a compelling way. This is the genius of using the word "God." It opens Israel's Scriptures in a more inclusive and universal way. It begins Genesis with a global vision. It leaves the reader/hearer wanting to know more. It allows Genesis to describe a different kind of God than the world has ever known. It leaves the reader open to hear the good news. It also models how to introduce others to the God who loves them. This, of course, means that this God desires to know you personally as well.

## Questions for Reflection

What are different names for God in our world today?

_____

_____

What do you mean by the word "God"?

_____

_____

What do you think or feel about the reality that the Creator God desires to know you?

_____

_____

# DAY 2

# The Shape of Creation

## Read Genesis 1:3–2:3

*And God said, "Let there be light," and there was light. God saw that
the light was good, and he separated the light from the darkness.
God called the light "day," and the darkness he called "night." And
there was evening, and there was morning—the first day.*

*And God said, "Let there be lights in the vault of the sky to separate the day
from the night, and let them serve as signs to mark seasons and days and
years, and let them be lights in the vault of the sky to give light on the earth."
And it was so. God made two great lights—the greater light to govern the
day and the lesser light to govern the night. He also made the stars. God
set them in the vault of the sky to give light on the earth, to govern the day
and the night, and to separate light from darkness. And God saw that it was
good. And there was evening, and there was morning—the fourth day.*

*Thus the heavens and the earth were completed in all their vast array.
By the seventh day God had finished the work he had been doing; so
on the seventh day he rested from all his work. Then God blessed the
seventh day and made it holy, because on it he rested from all the
work of creating that he had done.—Genesis 1:3–5, 14–19; 2:1–3*

---

**Core Truth:** God carefully crafted a very good world with humanity as
its highest expression and Sabbath rest as its climax.

---

Genesis 1:1 summarizes God's creative work: "In the beginning God
created the heavens and the earth." It declares that God made all that is.
The Scriptures from Genesis to Revelation tell a unified story of the God who

is both the Creator and the Savior. The Bible begins with creation to link the story of God's people with all creation. Beginning with Genesis 12, the Bible will focus on the beginnings of God's people: Israel. But first it connects Israel's story to the broader human story. God's people cannot be properly understood apart from their connection to the rest of humanity as well as to creation itself. If we want to understand our purpose in the world, we must understand God's original purposes in creation.

## The Pattern of Creation

Genesis 1:2–2:3 describes how God guided creation from a state of formlessness to goodness and Sabbath rest. Genesis uses a seven-day pattern to organize its description of creation.

Creation is a reflection of God's purposes. From the very beginning, God demonstrates a mission. God desires to move creation from disorder and formlessness in 1:2 to a place of beauty and order by 1:31. At the conclusion of each day, God evaluates his handiwork as "good." After God creates humanity and thereby finishes the work of creation, God declares it not merely "good," but "very good." This is emphatic language. The world that God created was *very good*. God always desires the best for creation and for us. This has been true from the moment that God spoke creation into existence.

God acts purposefully and alone to move creation to completion. Verse 2 marks the initial beginning of creation. Genesis 1:2 describes the chaotic state of the creation at its origin. In the creation stories of Israel's neighbors, creation emerged out of chaotic battles between the gods. In one story, the heavens and the earth were two halves of a goddess hacked into two pieces during one such battle. In Genesis, there is no hint of this. In fact, the biblical account is quiet and orderly. God acts unilaterally. The God of Genesis 1 does not need the permission of other deities, nor do other deities attempt to thwart his intentions. Creation is *good*, just as God willed it to be.

God creates by speaking the world into existence. The God of the Bible simply creates what he wills by commanding the various parts of creation into existence. God works to craft a very good universe. The biblical writer describes God's creative process in a way that enhances this portrayal of God in contrast to the haphazard, noisy, and chaotic creation accounts of Israel's neighbors.

## God Separates and Fills

Embedded in the six days of creation is a parallel structure between days 1–3 and days 4–6. In days 1–3, God separates and prepares the creation for life. In days 4–6, God fills this empty framework with objects, plants, animals, and people.

On day 1, God separates light from darkness; on day 3, God fills these spaces with the sun (the light during the day) and the moon and stars (lights during the night). The creation of the sun, moon, and stars is also a not-so-subtle declaration that these elements are not divine. Other nations worshiped these as deities. Genesis desires for us to worship only the invisible Creator God. Everything visible is simply part of the wondrous and good world that God made.

On day 2, God separates the waters above from the waters below; on day 5, God fills the waters above with birds and the waters below with fish. In the understanding of the ancients, the earth is surrounded by water. God creates a space for the land by separating the waters by means of a firmament or dome that prevents the waters above from falling. In this view of reality, the firmament or dome is the sky upon which the sun, moon, and stars (from day 4) move and in which the birds fly. The waters below are the oceans, rivers, streams, and springs in which the fish thrive and swim.

On day 3, God separates the waters below so that dry and inhabitable land can appear. God also commands the earth to send forth vegetation. By the end of day 3, God's good creation includes dry land covered with seed- and fruit-bearing trees. On the first part of day 6, God creates all the animals by commanding the earth to bring them forth. This is of course described as good, but God is not finished. He has one final act. On the second half of day 6, God pauses for a brief moment and then he forms humanity in his image. The invisible God will be made visible in only one part of creation: men and women. At this moment, creation is finished and the Creator looks down at the work of his hands. Creation is not merely good; it is now *very good*. God's creative activity ends with the creation of humanity to multiply, fill the earth, and serve as God's stewards over all creation.

## God Rests: Sabbath

The seventh day of creation contains a profound statement of God's inactivity. God's work is not the climax of creation; the true high point is God's Sabbath rest. The opening segment of Genesis (1:1–2:3) announces that the God who creates is also the God who rests. Moreover, God embeds Sabbath rest into the very framework of the universe that he crafted and formed. This is very good news indeed. In the following sections of this chapter, we will explore humanity as the high point of God's work and the climactic announcement of God's Sabbath rest.

## Questions for Reflection

What do you learn about God and the nature of our world from Genesis 1:1–2:3?

_____

_____

How would you describe the world that God made?

_____

_____

Is our world still "very good" today? Why or why not?

_____

_____

# DAY 3

# Humanity and the Image of God

Read Genesis 1:26–31; 2:4–25

*Then God said, "Let us make mankind in our image, in our likeness, so that they may rule over the fish in the sea and the birds in the sky, over the livestock and all the wild animals, and over all the creatures that move along the ground." So God created mankind in his own image, in the image of God he created them; male and female he created them. God blessed them and said to them, "Be fruitful and increase in number; fill the earth and subdue it. Rule over the fish in the sea and the birds in the sky and over every living creature that moves on the ground."—Genesis 1:26-28*

---

**Core Truth:** God creates all men and women in his image to serve as a missional community that reflects his character.

---

## Image and Mission

In 1:26–31, God creates humanity to make visible the invisible Creator. It is humanity alone that bears the image of God. Theologians use the Latin phrase *imago dei*. The word for image in Hebrew is *tselem*. It indicates a visible image or representation of something. The Old Testament often uses tselem to mean "idol." Idols served as visible representations of gods or goddesses. In the ancient world, great kings also would erect images of themselves across their realms. This allowed the king to project honor, glory, and power to those subjects who never saw him in person. Genesis 1:1–2:3 presents God as the Great King of creation. God is invisible and exists apart from his creation. On the sixth day, God crafts women and men to make the truth of his existence and character visible and tangible to all. It is humanity alone that serves

God by reflecting God's character. This is why the Bible is so adamant against worshiping anything but God or fashioning an idol to represent God. God created humans as his idols, or images, to make himself known to the rest of creation. At the heart of God forming us in his image is God's mission to reveal himself to all creation.

In Genesis 1:1–2:3, God creates the world as his cosmic temple. God is the Great King. Humanity serves as God's priests and visible representatives. In the Old Testament, priests connected others to God through sacred rituals and ordered the community through teaching God's ways. In Genesis 1:26–31, God crafts women and men for the mission of embodying his ways and modeling them for the rest of creation by serving the good of creation. This is the meaning of being made in the image of God. This is a mission worthy of our talents, passions, and lives.

## Image in All People

You can find other ancient writings that talk about humans in the image of God, but the Bible does it in the most radical way. When Israel's neighbors spoke of humanity in God's image, they typically affirmed that only the king bore God's image. In other words, Israel's neighbors used the image of God to grant privileges to the powerful (usually only the king) and to degrade the value of everyone else. The rest of humanity was reckoned to be slaves of the gods. Inequality is not part of Israel's vision of creation. The God of Genesis 1:1–2:3 has a different valuation of people. Humans are not mere afterthoughts or slaves of the gods. Instead, all humanity reflects the image of the Creator and thus has value and importance. There are no insignificant people or meaningless lives. Every human being has a role to play in God's mission. Profoundly, the Bible affirms against the grain of a male-dominated culture that women equally reflect God's image.

## Image as Community

Central to bearing God's image is humanity's creation as a *community*. In Genesis 1:1–2:3, only humanity is explicitly created male and female. This is important. God created us for community. God creates men and women in his image to serve as a missional community. Genesis 1:26–31 describes humanity's mission to serve as stewards of creation. They fulfill this role by filling the earth with other men and women. God desires to have visible representations of his character and purposes spread across the world reflecting God to all creation.

## Humanity at the Center of God's Plans

Genesis 2:4–25 builds on the story of 1:26–31. It is in 2:4 that we first learn the name of God. Our translations typically read "LORD God." This is a traditional way of translating *Yahweh Elohim*. Always remember that when you read "LORD" in the Old Testament that it is God's personal name and not a formal title. If Genesis 1:1–2:3 raised the question of the true identity of God, 2:4 proclaims that God's name is the LORD (Yahweh).

Genesis 2:4–25 reaffirms humanity's mission of caring for creation. Adam demonstrates humanity's stewardship and dominion over creation by naming the animals (2:19–20). Dominion does not give humans the right to abuse or neglect creation. Humanity is to serve rather than exploit. It is a dominion through service rather than through domination. The language of "work it and take care of it" in Genesis 2:15 indicates a level of creativity and enhancement of God's creation.

In Genesis 2, the creation of the first woman takes center stage. God affirms the importance of community, saying, "It is not good for the man to be alone" (2:18). God creates a partner (helper) for man. Helper is not a subservient role for women. In fact, in the majority of occurrences of "helper" (Hebrew *'ezer*) in the Old Testament, God is the helper (see Ps. 121). If God can be called Israel's helper, then this role is certainly not a demeaning or lesser role in any way. The union of man and his partner brings Genesis 2 to a conclusion (2:23–25). Their relationship is beautiful and models authentic community rooted in equality, harmony, peace, and mutuality.

## A Holy Missional Community

God creates humanity to serve as a missional community that reflects his character to the rest of creation. As we seek to realign with God, we must take seriously mission, community, and character. In fact, Jesus came to announce the kingdom as the means to call women and men to their true humanity.

This is good news, but there is still more. We will move to the full climax of creation: God's gift of Sabbath.

## Questions for Reflection

What does it mean to be human according to Genesis 1–2?

_____

_____

How does our culture's view of humanity contrast with the biblical view?

_____

_____

How does this text call you to live out mission as part of a community that reflects God's character?

_____

_____

# DAY 4

# The Gift of the Sabbath

Read Genesis 2:1–3; Exodus 20:8–11

*"Remember the Sabbath day by keeping it holy. Six days you shall labor and do all your work, but the seventh day is a sabbath to the LORD your God. On it you shall not do any work, neither you, nor your son or daughter, nor your male or female servant, nor your animals, nor any foreigner residing in your towns. For in six days the LORD made the heavens and the earth, the sea, and all that is in them, but he rested on the seventh day. Therefore the LORD blessed the Sabbath day and made it holy.—Exodus 20:8–11*

> **Core Truth:** The climax of creation is God's resting on the Sabbath day. God extends this blessing to all creation.

After God forms humanity and pronounces creation "very good," God rests. How many of us *rest*? Modern life is filled with complex and multiple demands. Yet the Bible begins by asserting that Sabbath rest is the climax of the creation. Life is not designed to be endless toil. Even the most life-affirming activities must cease for Sabbath. God's work of creation moved the universe from emptiness (1:2) to very goodness (1:31) to Sabbath rest (2:1–3). Sabbath is God's final gift to the creation.

## Sabbath and God

God works. God rests. This establishes a key rhythm for understanding life. Ponder this: our Creator rests. This is a radically different world from the one we find today. Most of us race daily from one activity to another. We are tired. Some of us work long hours for little pay. Others are exhausted due to the weight of unemployment and the financial challenges that come with it.

Yet Genesis 2:1–3 offers us a portrait of abundance. God rests. Moreover, God blesses this day of rest and makes it holy (2:3). This means that God has set apart a sacred space and time for rest. Profoundly, God shares this rest with us by extending Sabbath to all creation. Sabbath serves as a principle for establishing justice and good in the world. Unlike other ancient creation stories, such as the Babylonian *Atrahasis* where humans exist merely to serve as slaves for the gods, the LORD demonstrates his ultimate goodness with the gift of Sabbath. Jesus will later remind us of this reality in the New Testament: "The Sabbath was made for people, not people for the Sabbath" (Mark 2:27).

## Sabbath and Life

Sabbath is a core principle for ordering our spiritual, personal, and social lives. It connects us with the world around us. Later in the Old Testament, God's Sabbath will be the key commandment for linking love for God with love for neighbor. In the Ten Commandments (Exod. 20:1–17 and Deut. 5:6–21), the command to honor and keep Sabbath is the longest and most detailed of the commands. It serves as the bridge between the commandments focusing on our relationship with God (i.e., other gods, idols, dishonoring of God's name) and the commandments rooted in our relating with others (i.e., honoring parents, stealing, murder, adultery, false witness, coveting). Sabbath has all creation in view. Humanity stops its work and rests. This rest includes all of one's family, all of one's employees or servants, and even all of one's animals. Sabbath is a community practice. There is no solitary Sabbath in Scripture. God rests and so does his creation.

## Sabbath in the Old Testament

Throughout the Old Testament, the Sabbath pattern of six days of work and a seventh day of rest repeats and foreshadows God's abundant future. In Exodus and Leviticus, the Sabbath principle establishes protections for humanity and creation. Slavery is regulated so that slaves are released after six years of service (Exod. 21:1–11). Agricultural lands receive a sabbath rest every seventh year (Exod. 23:10–11). These regulations point to God's broader vision for justice in his world. Obviously, slaves were among the most marginalized populations in the ancient world. Most slaves in ancient Israel became slaves as a means of paying off debts in an economy lacking modern bankruptcy protection. It is profound that the Bible confronted this tragic reality directly by offering real protections for those forced into slavery. Likewise, the resting of fields involved more than crop rotation. The sabbath rest for the fields served to provide food for the poor and for the animal world.

The book of Leviticus includes a bold vision for a once-in-a-generation economic reboot (see Lev. 25). After seven cycles of seven years, God expected his people to celebrate the year of Jubilee. In Jubilee, creditors forgave all debts, sold property was returned to its original owners, and slaveholders released slaves. Jubilee demonstrated God's justice and goodness. Thus, Sabbath points to the good life. We may find ourselves in difficult circumstances and trying times, but God's rest awaits us.

## Living the Sabbath Today

Sabbath is a radical concept. We live in a 24/7 world. Sabbath challenges the busy-ness of life. What if the most profound act you could do is to be fully present and do nothing? Rest is not a means to some end; rest is the end. God moves creation from emptiness to very goodness and then rests. God doesn't rest so that he can work. God works so that he can rest. Rest is the final word. This signals something profound about life. The meaning of life cannot simply be reduced to what we do. Work is valuable. Mission is important. Community is critical. Holiness is necessary. Yet the climax of creation is a time carved out for rest in communion with God. Think about the witness that such a bold and daring time of inaction would offer to a world trapped in endless cycles of busy-ness and the chaos of over-commitment. Sabbath is a declaration of faith that our present and future does not depend on our actions but on God's.

As we read the Bible together, we will continue to talk about our role in God's mission. But the challenge of Sabbath is that God rested and so must we. The Jesus who calls us to serve as a missional community also invites us to Sabbath: "Come to me, all you who are weary and burdened, and I will give you rest" (Matt. 11:28).

## Questions for Reflection

What does Sabbath teach us about God's mission?

_____

_____


How would you need to change in order to embrace a real Sabbath in your life?

_____

_____

# DAY 5

# Jesus and New Creation

### Read John 1:1–18; 2 Corinthians 5:16–21

*The Word became flesh and made his dwelling among us. We have seen his glory, the glory of the one and only Son, who came from the Father, full of grace and truth. (John testified concerning him. He cried out, saying, "This is he of whom I said, 'He who comes after me has surpassed me because he was before me.'") Out of his fullness we have all received grace in place of grace already given. For the law was given through Moses; grace and truth came through Jesus Christ. No one has ever seen God, but the one and only Son, who is himself God and is in closest relationship with the Father, has made him known.—John 1:14–18*

---

**Core Truth:** Jesus comes to model the truly human life and to make it possible for us to live as the people whom God created us to be.

---

Genesis 1–2 sets the stage for the rest of the biblical story by describing the very good world that God made. It paints a picture of the world as God intended it to be.

The story of Scripture from Genesis 12 through the book of Revelation focuses on God's work of healing his creation and reconciling humanity to himself. We will discover that the Bible's vision of creation remains a core theme as God works toward a New Creation. We'll say much more about this when we get to the New Testament, but let's look briefly at two New Testament passages: John 1:1–18 and 2 Corinthians 5:16–21.

## John 1:1–18

John's Gospel opens with words chosen to bring to mind the first words of Genesis: "In the beginning was the Word, and the Word was with God, and the

Word was God." John's prologue is rich in imagery and thick in meaning. John uses a philosophical concept made popular by the first-century Jewish writer Philo. Philo described God's word active in creation as the Word (in Greek, *logos*). Logos, or Word, referred to God's agent of creation. Remarkably, John identifies the logos of creation with the pre-incarnate Jesus. Thus, John draws from a popular idea in his day to link Jesus the Messiah with God's creative acts in Genesis 1. Jesus, the one through whom God announced the kingdom, was present from eternity and served as the agent of creation. From Genesis to the witness of the Gospels, the Bible affirms that the Creator and the Savior are one and the same. The God who creates a very good world is also the God who acts to save and redeem his creation.

By echoing Genesis 1:1, John also denies an often-believed assumption about the Bible. One often hears that the God of the Old Testament is radically different than the God of the New Testament. John confronts this directly by asserting that the God of the Old Testament manifests his character and identity most fully in Jesus. John goes on to say, "The Word became flesh and made his dwelling among us" (John 1:14). What is Jesus' role on earth? Jesus comes to show us the truth about God. The fullest expression of God takes on human flesh and blood.

John also writes, "No one has ever seen God, but the one and only Son, who is himself God and is in closest relationship with the Father, has made him known" (John 1:18). God the Creator is invisible. Yet God desires to be known. In Genesis 1:1–2:3, God made human beings in his image for the purpose of making himself known to creation. Due to the failure of people to live out this mission, Jesus fulfills God's intentions for humanity.

## 2 Corinthians 5:16–21

In 2 Corinthians 5:17, Paul writes: "Therefore, if anyone is in Christ, the new creation has come: The old has gone, the new is here!" Paul profoundly states the reality of the work of Jesus for us. The life, death, and resurrection of Jesus is the climactic act of God's plan of salvation. Through Jesus, God gives the gift of reconciliation. Through Jesus, God offers humanity the opportunity to become the man or the woman whom God created us to be. We can experience new creation. Jesus came to make us human again. Jesus works to restore us to serve as God's people. Paul speaks of new creation in Christ and immediately links it with mission through our roles as ambassadors. An ambassador represents a ruler and kingdom while living in a foreign land. The true king is not present so the ambassador speaks and acts on his behalf. Is this role sounding familiar? Paul uses slightly different terminology but his vision for new life in Christ is in harmony with God's original creational purposes for humanity. In Christ, we can be restored to be God's missional community that reflects God's character in/to/for the world.

## Creation and Faith

We are getting ahead of our story a bit by jumping ahead to the New Testament. But this gives us a sneak peak of what is to come. As we seek to find ourselves in the biblical story, let us remember two key elements from our brief look at creation.

First, this world is the avenue of God's mission. God creates it and pronounces it "very good." As we will see, it has become fractured and infested by sin, but it remains the focus of God's activity. Following Jesus is not an escape from this world but a commissioning to Jesus' mission to bring hope, healing, and reconciliation.

Second, all human beings are created in the image of God and have dignity, worth, and value. Thus, following Jesus means practicing justice through the love and service of all people. The Christ-following movement must not be restricted to any ethnicity, socio-economic grouping, or region. Just as the book of Genesis opens with all the world in view, following Jesus involves an openness to the world and a desire to see God's kingdom manifest globally. The kingdom is good news for everyone, or it's not good news for anyone. We are blessed by God to be a blessing to others.

## Questions for Reflection

How does Jesus' mission relate to God's original creation?

_____

_____

What would it look like to live as a new creation in your neighborhood today?

_____

_____

# Creation and the Mission of God

## CORE TRUTHS

1. Creation stories teach us about God, the world, and ourselves.
2. God carefully crafted a very good world with humanity as its highest expression and Sabbath rest as its climax.
3. God creates all men and women in his image to serve as a missional community that reflects his character.
4. The climax of creation is God's resting on the Sabbath day. God extends this blessing to all creation.
5. Jesus comes to model the truly human life and to make it possible for us to live as the people whom God created us to be.

## OPEN SESSION WITH PRAYER

Welcome the group and give new participants the opportunity to introduce themselves.

## DEBRIEF THE READING FOR THE WEEK (15 MINUTES)

- What were the key takeaways that you gained from this week's reading?
- What aspects of the reading did you find confusing?
- How does the intended world as described in Genesis contrast with our present world?
- How does the Bible's message of creation challenge our understanding of the world and the value of all people?
- What does it mean to be created in God's image?

## WATCH VIDEO (30 MINUTES)

## CONVERSATION (15 MINUTES)

- What aspects of Brian's message resonated with you most deeply?
- What questions did the video raise for you?
- What does the message of creation teach us about God and his mission?
- In what ways are you living as the person whom God created you to be?
- How does the Bible present Jesus as the way to life as God intended it to be?
- What would it look like to live as a new creation in your neighborhood today?
- Who in your life needs to hear the good news of the Bible?

## CLOSING PRAYER

## CHAPTER THREE

# Paradise Lost

The very good world that God created is not the world in which we live today. The biblical story moves from describing life as God intended to narrating the principal problem facing God's creation: sin and brokenness. Human sin results in a fractured creation, guilt, broken relationships, and lostness. The good news is that from the moment of sin's entrance into the world, God demonstrates his love and commitment to his creation by working to bring wholeness and reconciliation to it. God's plan of salvation will reach its climax in the life, death, and resurrection of Jesus.

# DAY 1

# The Garden

Read Genesis 3:1–8; Romans 5:12–21

*Now the serpent was more crafty than any of the wild animals the LORD God*
*had made. He said to the woman, "Did God really say, 'You must not eat*
*from any tree in the garden'?" The woman said to the serpent, "We may eat*
*fruit from the trees in the garden, but God did say, 'You must not eat fruit*
*from the tree that is in the middle of the garden, and you must not touch it,*
*or you will die.'" "You will not certainly die," the serpent said to the woman.*
*"For God knows that when you eat of it your eyes will be opened, and you*
*will be like God, knowing good and evil." When the woman saw that the fruit*
*of the tree was good for food and pleasing to the eye, and also desirable for*
*gaining wisdom, she took some and ate it. She also gave some to her husband,*
*who was with her, and he ate it. Then the eyes of both of them were opened,*
*and they realized they were naked; so they sewed fig leaves together and*
*made coverings for themselves. Then the man and his wife heard the sound*
*of the LORD God as he was walking in the garden in the cool of the day, and*
*they hid from the LORD God among the trees of the garden.—Genesis 3:1–8*

---

**Core Truth:** Sin and human brokenness result from our inability to
trust that God has our best interests in his heart.

---

In Genesis 3–11, human sin and brokenness shatter the profound potential
of God's very good creation (Gen 1–2). Our world today is not the world as
God intended. Instead it is scarred by sin due to the choices and consequences
of people acting apart from God's designs. Genesis 3–11 serves the scriptural
story by narrating the fall of humanity and creation. It is the problem that the
gospel solves.

The story of the fall begins with a conversation between the first humans and a talking snake. Genesis does not provide background on the snake. It is part of creation. In tradition, the snake is often associated with Satan, but ancient readers would not have immediately made that connection. The snake does not have any special powers or abilities other than speech. It challenges the authority and character of God, but it will be the choices of men and women that bring sin and brokenness to God's very good creation.

The snake begins by asking a question of Eve, "Did God really say, 'You must not eat from any tree in the garden'?" (Gen. 3:1). The opening words provide a pivotal moment in history. So far in Genesis, humans interacted with God directly. Now something has changed. The German theologian Dietrich Bonhoeffer called these verses the "first conversation about God."[5] God has become object rather than subject. This is a reminder for us as we read God's Word together. Is God an object that we study? Or is God the subject of our lives? Do we study the Bible to gain knowledge or to listen to God's voice? Do we practice religious acts out of tradition or do we embrace a moment-by-moment relationship with God?

The biblical story would be radically different if Eve had immediately replied, "Let's ask him." Eve doesn't do this, so the conversation continues. The snake challenges Eve's knowledge of God by questioning his commands. The serpent cites the only prohibition that God gave the first humans. In Genesis 2:16–17, God prohibited humanity from eating from the tree of the knowledge of good and evil. If they ate it, they would die. The serpent changes the original command slightly asking, "Did God really say, 'You must not eat from any tree in the garden'?" (3:1). Eve recognizes the error and immediately corrects the snake. They can eat from all trees except for one. She also adds that they were not to touch it. The significance of Eve's addition is debatable. Perhaps it was an extra safeguard. The problem is that the serpent has her on the wrong road because she is talking about rules rather than the relationship humanity enjoys with God.

God has become the object rather than the subject. In verses 4–5, the serpent asserts contrary to God that Eve will not die. God is lying, according to the serpent. Moreover, he asserts that God forbids them from eating from the tree out of a selfish desire to prevent Eve from acquiring something desirable and good: the wisdom to discern good and evil *just as God can*. This is the real temptation. It is not a trick by the serpent. It is a choice that confronts Eve and

Adam. God has already granted humanity a central role in his mission. God creates humanity to be his visible representatives. They are to fill the earth and live as God's agents of blessing. The serpent suggests that humanity's privileged position is, in reality, a confining box. Implied is a bold assertion: God cannot be trusted and does not have humanity's best interests at heart. God is selfishly withholding something good from humanity. The lesson: once God is made an object, it is easy for us to begin to doubt and lose trust.

Do I trust that God has my best interest at heart? This is a burning question that we must ask ourselves just as Eve and Adam did. And if we cannot trust God, whom can we trust? The answer is easy. We trust ourselves. We act out of our strengths, talents, and experiences. Eve eats the fruit *because she trusts herself more than she trusts that God has her best interests at heart*. Ponder Eve's thought process: "the fruit of the tree was good for food and pleasing to the eye, and also desirable for gaining wisdom, she took some and ate it" (3:6). Genesis 2:9 tells us that every tree in the garden is good for food and pleasing to the eye. Thus the phrase "desirable for gaining wisdom" is the real motivation. Eve and Adam willingly disobey God because they want something that God did not intend for them to have. They chose to move beyond the boundaries God established.

Oswald Chambers, in his classic devotional *My Utmost for His Highest*, defined sin as "my claim to my right to myself."[6] The human story repeatedly witnesses to our choosing our own way rather than God's. Tragically, this is the way of death. It has plagued humanity since the garden. Paul summarizes this in his letter to the Romans 5:12, "Therefore, just as sin entered the world through one man, and death through sin, and in this way death came to all people because all sinned."

Eve and Adam both eat. Traditionally it is thought that Eve carries the blame for this first act of disobedience. However, in Genesis 3:6, Adam is with Eve and has been with her for the entire scene. The sin in the garden is the sin of Adam and Eve. But it is important to move beyond looking for blame. The true power of this story is what it says about us. Sin is the *problem* of every human person. In Romans 3:23, Paul categorically writes, "for all have sinned and fall short of the glory of God" (cf. Eph. 2:1–2).

## Questions for Reflection

Do you trust that God has your best interest at heart?

_____

_____

Do you trust that God has the best interests of the people you love in his heart?

_____

_____

How would your life be different if you fully trusted God right now?

_____

_____

# DAY 2

# Good-Bye to Eden

## Read Genesis 3:9–16

*But the Lord God called to the man, "Where are you?" He answered, "I heard you in the garden, and I was afraid because I was naked; so I hid." And he said, "Who told you that you were naked? Have you eaten from the tree that I commanded you not to eat from?" The man said, "The woman you put here with me—she gave me some fruit from the tree, and I ate it." Then the Lord God said to the woman, "What is this you have done?" The woman said, "The serpent deceived me, and I ate." So the Lord God said to the serpent, "Because you have done this, Cursed are you above all livestock and all wild animals! You will crawl on your belly and you will eat dust all the days of your life. And I will put enmity between you and the woman, and between your offspring and hers; he will crush your head, and you will strike his heel." To the woman he said, "I will make your pains in childbearing very severe; with painful labor you will give birth to children. Your desire will be for your husband, and he will rule over you."—Genesis 3:9–16*

---

**Core Truth:** Sin damages our relationships with God, other people, and creation.

---

The results of Adam and Eve's fateful decision are instantaneous. They desired a higher wisdom and ended up ashamed over their nakedness (3:10). They had believed wrongly that eating the forbidden fruit would enhance their lives. Tragically, instead, it limited their future choices. Adam and Eve experienced separation from each other. Their awareness of their own nakedness caused them to hide their own bodies from one another. This is a far cry from their previous intimacy in Genesis 2:24–25, "This is why a man leaves his father and mother and is united to his wife, and they become one flesh. Adam and his wife were both naked, and they felt no shame." But this is merely the beginning of the havoc that sin unleashes. If Genesis 1–2 presented a very good creation, Genesis 3–11 traces the brokenness and loss that comes with sin. In Genesis 1–2, men and women enjoyed rich and full relationships with God, the rest of creation, and each other. Sin damages all of these relationships.

Adam and Eve are also ashamed to be seen by their Creator. They hear God taking his daily walk through the garden on his way to fellowshipping with them, and they hide. This is what sin and brokenness do. It creates a breach in our relationship with God. But note the cause of the fracture. God does not hide from Adam and Eve. Of all the actions that God could have taken in response to human disobedience, God chose to seek out his prized creation. God calls out, "Where are you? (Gen. 3:9). Don't miss this. Sin causes humanity to hide from God; it doesn't cause God to turn away and hide from us. God immediately comes looking for his lost man and woman. "Where are you?" is one of the most tragic yet profound lines in Scripture. It is tragic because humanity was created to be in relationship with God and now it flees from this privilege. It is truly good news because God continues to desire relationship despite humanity's disobedience. This is the heart of the gospel and its first echo. God will work from Genesis 3 forward to bring reconciliation and wholeness to humanity.

Sin has consequences. It creates brokenness, shame, alienation, and lostness. When God finds Adam and Eve, they are far from wise as a result of eating the fruit. In the remainder of Genesis 3, we encounter the reversal of the beauty and relational wholeness of God's original creation. The tight-knit community between Adam and Eve is gone. The perception of their nakedness separates them; they make it worse by resorting to blame—Adam blames Eve, and Eve blames the serpent (3:12–13). Rather than living together in mutuality and harmony as God intended, Adam and Eve will now compete against each other for supremacy. They will desire to control one another rather than love and build one another up (3:16).

The final consequence is the damage that extends to creation. Humanity was created to practice faithful stewardship of God's world (Gen. 1:26–31; 2:15). Now this mission becomes more difficult. Humanity will no longer have ease in its interaction with creation. The work of securing food will be toilsome. Rather than a fertile garden full of abundant and delicious meals, men and women will find thorns and thistles (3:17–19). Scripture does not detail how sin fractures the creation as a whole, but it affirms this reality. God's original purpose for humanity was a mission of stewarding the created world. Now creation has lost its steward. In Romans 8:19–22, Paul describes the longing of creation for redemption:

> For the creation waits in eager expectation for the children of God to be revealed. For the creation was subjected to frustration, not by its own choice, but by the will of the one who subjected it, in hope that the creation itself will be liberated from its bondage to decay and brought into the freedom and glory of the children of God. We know that the whole creation has been groaning as in the pains of childbirth right up to the present time.

At the end of Genesis 3, God graciously covers the perceived nakedness and shame of Adam and Eve with garments of skin (3:21). This demonstrates God's ongoing commitment and care for humanity. But there is also a final consequence of sin—God exiles humanity from Eden (3:23). In its attempt to break out of the boundaries created by God for human life to thrive, humanity loses access to the tree of life and now faces life (and eventually death) as wanderers on the earth. Genesis 3 asks us a fundamental question of trust: Do we trust that God has our best interests at heart as well as those of the persons we love? This trust question is a watershed for us. Its answer is critical for our journey through this world.

## Questions for Reflection

What do we learn about God from his response to the sin of humanity?

_____

_____

Who do you know that might desperately need to know about a God who responds to human brokenness with a desire to restore the relationship?

_____

_____

# DAY 3

# Sin—The Next Generations

### Read Genesis 4:1–16, 25–26; 5:1–8, 21–24, 28–32

*Adam made love to his wife Eve, and she became pregnant and gave birth to Cain. She said, "With the help of the LORD I have brought forth a man." Later she gave birth to his brother Abel. Now Abel kept flocks, and Cain worked the soil. In the course of time Cain brought some of the fruits of the soil as an offering to the LORD. And Abel also brought an offering—fat portions from some of the firstborn of his flock. The LORD looked with favor on Abel and his offering, but on Cain and his offering he did not look with favor. So Cain was very angry, and his face was downcast. Then the LORD said to Cain, "Why are you angry? Why is your face downcast? If you do what is right, will you not be accepted? But if you do not do what is right, sin is crouching at your door; it desires to have you, but you must rule over it." Now Cain said to his brother Abel, "Let's go out to the field." While they were in the field, Cain attacked his brother Abel and killed him.—Genesis 4:1–8*

*Adam made love to his wife again, and she gave birth to a son and named him Seth, saying, "God has granted me another child in place of Abel, since Cain killed him." Seth also had a son, and he named him Enosh. At that time people began to call on the name of the LORD.—Genesis 4:25–26*

---

**Core Truth:** Sin infests and infects all people, relationships, institutions, and creation itself.

---

When we talk about the fall of humanity, we often focus our attention only on the garden story of Genesis 3. It does narrate the beginnings of human lostness, but it gets worse. Sin infests and infects.

## Cain and Abel

Genesis 4 opens positively. God exiled Adam and Eve out of Eden, but they are very much alive. In fact, they are now the parents of two sons, Cain and Abel. This should be a sign of hope, but their names foreshadow a continuation of trouble. In Hebrew, the name Cain sounds like a word meaning "brought forth." At Cain's birth, Eve exclaims, "With the help of the LORD I have brought forth a man" (4:1). In Genesis 3, we already witnessed the tragic result of humanity going beyond its boundaries. Eve's announcement acknowledges God, yet puts the focus on her power and action in creation. If Cain's name points to human power, Abel's points to low expectations. Abel sounds like the word meaning "breath" or "vanity."

The rest of the story is well known. God accepts Abel's offering; God rejects Cain's. Cain becomes so angry and disenchanted that he murders his younger brother. In the garden, sin caused fractured relationships. Now we have murder.

What does this story mean? First, it doesn't tell us why God accepts only Abel's offering. Later in Scripture, there will be both animal and first-fruit offerings (see Lev. 1–7 and Deut. 26:1–11). There may be a cultural message here. Ancient people privileged the firstborn. By accepting the younger son's offering, God offers the good news that blessings are available to all and that the future will arrive through God's ways of service and sacrifice rather than through birthright, power, affluence, or cunning.

Second, Genesis 3 and 4 offer insights on avoiding sin. In Genesis 2–3, God gave Adam and Eve commands about the forbidden fruit. Adam and Eve knew the prohibition but disregarded it. In Genesis 4:6–7, God arrives to dissuade Cain *before* he acts. God offers Cain an out, but Cain ignores God and kills his brother. Scripture is clear that all people sin, but sin is a choice that people make.

Third, God continues to engage humanity despite its sin. God arrives on the scene after the fateful act and investigates. This results in further alienation. God pushes Cain out deeper into the world. Sin fractures the human family. Yet God still protects Cain as he wanders about living as a sojourner "east of Eden" (4:16). Sin has consequences, but God continues to work to restore relationships and redeem his lost people.

## Cain and a New Hope

The human saga advances as Genesis traces seven generations of Cain's descendants. Cain's violence tragically continues and reaches comic proportions with Lamech, who boasts to his wives of his violent and vengeful ways: "Adah and Zillah, listen to me; wives of Lamech, hear my words. I have killed a man for wounding me, a young man for injuring me. If Cain is avenged seven times, then Lamech seventy-seven times" (4:23–24).

Profoundly, 4:25–26 offers a glimmer of hope. Adam and Eve have a new son named Seth. Seth means "granted." Unlike the boasting accompanying Cain's birth, Eve receives Seth as a gift from God. All we know of Seth is this report in 4:26: "At that time people began to call on the name of the LORD." This is the first place in Scripture post-garden where humanity actively seeks God. This suggests that there is always an alternative path to sin, violence, brokenness, alienation, and pride.

## Death, Life, and Hope

In Genesis 5, we encounter the first long genealogy in the Bible. The ancients found truth in genealogies. Inside the list of strange names are lessons to shape God's people. In Genesis 5, people lived for hundreds of years. Claims of extraordinary lifespans are common in the literature of the biblical world. For example, the Sumerian King's List, which dates from about 2000 BC, describes the reigns of kings before and after the flood. Some who reigned before the flood ruled for more than twenty thousand years. Such numbers make Methuselah's 969 years appear unremarkable (5:27).

The real story in Genesis 5 is the recurrence of "and then he died." Death is the final word. Underneath Israel's memory of extraordinary lifespans is the harsh reality of life's finiteness. God created us for eternity but sin results in death.

Yet in this context of death is a word of good news. The seventh generation from Adam is Enoch (Gen. 5:21–24). Enoch lives for 365 years, but he does not die. Both 7 and 365 are symbols of completeness. He lives a complete life because he "walked faithfully with God" (v. 24). This key phrase in Genesis describes faithful people. This language will also be used of Noah and Abraham (6:10 and 17:1 respectively). "Walk faithfully" indicates a life lived for God.

Enoch contrasts with all who came before him, but in particular he contrasts with Lamech, the seventh generation from Cain. Lamech embodies the worst traits of humanity: violence and vengeance; Enoch *walks faithfully with God.* God rewards him by taking him away. Enoch leaves this world to be with God. Thus, we find a *hopeful* alternative for humanity. Dust is not the only option. As we move through Scripture, hope will increase.

The genealogy ends on another hopeful note with the birth of Noah. Noah sounds like the Hebrew word for "comfort." Noah will bring comfort. Noah's father blesses him saying, "He will comfort us in the labor and painful toil of our hands caused by the ground the LORD has cursed" (5:29). Perhaps the line of Seth will indeed begin to reverse the devastating effects of sin and human brokenness.

## Questions for Reflection

In what ways do we see the brokenness of Genesis 3–5 in our world today?

_____

_____

As you reflect on the trajectory of your own life, do you want to be part of the problem or part of the solution?

_____

_____

How would your life need to be different to be part of God's mission?

_____

_____

# DAY 4

# Noah and the Great Flood

Read Genesis 6:1–13; 7:17–8:5; 9:8–17

*Then God said to Noah and to his sons with him: "I now establish my covenant with you and with your descendants after you and with every living creature that was with you—the birds, the livestock and all the wild animals, all those that came out of the ark with you— every living creature on earth. I establish my covenant with you: Never again will all life be destroyed by the waters of a flood; never again will there be a flood to destroy the earth."—Genesis 9:8-11*

> **Core Truth:** Despite the sinfulness of humanity and the corruption of creation's original goodness, God acts to save a remnant of humanity (Noah and his family) and issues a promise that guarantees the future of God's creation.

Genesis 6–9 tells the story of Noah and the great flood. This story raises difficult questions. How is it possible for a flood so epic that it could cover the entire world? What kind of a god would kill every living creature except for a single family and a few animals?

But Noah's story contains good news and shows the LORD God to be a different god than the gods of the nations. Just as with the creation stories, Noah's story serves as a witness to the reality, power, and kindness of the true God. It is a story of hope and points to the good news of a God who cares for his creation. Instead of focusing on modern questions such as, "Did it really happen?" or "Why would a loving God destroy the earth?" we will read Noah's story through the eyes of the ancients to see how it functions in the narrative of God's mission of redeeming us from our lostness.

## Ancient Flood Stories

Israel's neighbors, including the Sumerians, Assyrians, and Babylonians, recorded accounts of great floods sent to punish and destroy humanity.

In these accounts, the gods are mean and vindictive. In the Babylonian *Atrahasis*, the gods send a flood to destroy humanity simply because of humanity's *noisiness*. The gods destroy the world but they lose control of the flood. In fact, the destructive power of the flood frightens the gods. The flood devastates humanity except for Atrahasis (and his family), who had been warned and built a boat. Ironically, the gods grow hungry as the world lacks people to offer sacrifices. When Atrahasis disembarks from his ark and offers a sacrifice, the gods flock to it. In the aftermath, the gods decide on a different approach to human noise. One-third of all women will not be able to give birth. There will be enough people to offer sacrifices without all of the noise! There is no gospel here—vindictive gods who can't control their own power, humans as slaves, and one-third of couples unable to have children.

## Noah and God

Against this context, Genesis 6–9 is a witness to the LORD. In Genesis, God acts consistently according to his character. Previously, we've seen his kindness to Adam, Eve, and Cain following their sins. In Genesis 6, sin is again the problem. Humanity continues in willful disobedience. Genesis 6:1–4 describes the illegitimate mixing between heavenly beings and humans. Humanity continues to violate God-given limits. Genesis 6:5–8 offers God's evaluation of humanity. In Genesis 1:1–2:3, God formed a "very good" creation. There is no such evaluation in Genesis 6. God observes humanity and offers a tragic assessment: "The LORD saw how great the wickedness of the human race had become on the earth, and that every inclination of the thoughts of the human heart was only evil all the time" (6:5). Yet God responds with sorrow and grief over the evil of humanity (6:6). This is no portrait of an enraged god of wrath. Genesis 6:11–13 repeats some of the details of 6:5–8, but includes a summative assessment of the created world. All flesh (animal and human) is corrupt in the post-garden world of Noah's day.

But there was one exception—Noah. Noah found favor with God because Noah was *righteous* and *blameless*. Genesis 6:9 informs us that Noah "walked faithfully with God." This is the same language used to describe Enoch (5:24). Noah is singled out not for ability or intellect but by *character*. God reveals his intention to reboot creation by destroying all living creatures. God exhorts Noah to craft an ark to protect his family and preserve samples of all animals and birds. Noah faithfully follows God's instructions. He loads his family and the animals into the ark and God sends forty days and nights of flooding. Unlike in *Atrahasis*, God remains in control. The events unfold according to the will of God. Genesis 8:1 captures a key moment. After the waters stop, the earth remains flooded for one hundred fifty days. At this point, 8:1 reads, "But God remembered Noah." Rather than suggesting a lapse in God's memory, *remembered* signals God actively moving to *deliver* Noah from the waters. The LORD is a saving God. Judgment is not his final verdict. He has a mission. Humanity's sin disrupted God's creational intentions, but God's mission will prevail. After the earth dries, Noah, his family, and the animals disembark to repopulate the earth. Noah builds an altar and offers a sacrifice to God. In response, God promises to never again destroy the earth by flood. God will find a different way of redeeming the world.

## Key Lessons from Noah

Noah's story speaks to the lostness of humanity. It offers a rich understanding of human sin. It serves equally to remind us that there will be people who will respond positively to God. Noah was the *solitary* righteous man in his day, but the point is: *there was at least one*. Noah's story teaches us about God. God is relational. Humanity's sin grieves God, but God continues to reach out. He is different from other gods. He acts alone. He holds sway over creation and can control the great waters. Most profound, God is a god of salvation. Although there is only a single faithful human, God acts to save him and work through him to preserve a remnant through which God will replenish the earth. This contrasts with the flood stories of other nations in which the gods act vindictively due to there being too many noisy humans.

Noah's story ends with God establishing a covenant with Noah. This is the first covenant in Scripture. A covenant is a formal agreement between two parties. God uses covenant to help communicate the reality of his relational commitment to humanity. Noah's covenant is God's gift to *all* living creatures. God is pro-creation. God pledges a new path forward. The future is secure for all creation to prosper. God's mission will work to redeem *this* creation rather than destroy it. This is good news.

## Questions for Reflection

What is the good news in the story of Noah?

_____

_____

How is the LORD different from other gods according to Noah's story?

_____

_____

# DAY 5

# Human Corruption and God's Mission

## Read Genesis 10:32; 11:1–26

*Now the whole world had one language and a common speech. As people moved eastward, they found a plain in Shinar and settled there. They said to each other, "Come, let's make bricks and bake them thoroughly." They used brick instead of stone, and tar for mortar. Then they said, "Come, let us build ourselves a city, with a tower that reaches to the heavens, so that we may make a name for ourselves; otherwise we will be scattered over the face of the whole earth." But the LORD came down to see the city and the tower the people were building. The LORD said, "If as one people speaking the same language they have begun to do this, then nothing they plan to do will be impossible for them. Come, let us go down and confuse their language so they will not understand each other." So the LORD scattered them from there over all the earth, and they stopped building the city. That is why it was called Babel—because there the LORD confused the language of the whole world. From there the LORD scattered them over the face of the whole earth.—Genesis 11:1–9*

> **Core Truth:** By the end of Genesis 11, God's mission reaches a watershed moment as a lost humanity has filled the earth and stands in desperate need of salvation.

By Genesis 11:26, we find ourselves in a remarkable place. In alignment with God's creational vision, humanity has filled the earth. God has achieved his desire to have visible representations of himself all over creation.

But the critical problem is human sin. Humanity fills the earth, but humanity has demonstrated its persistent unfaithfulness.

## The Table of the Nations and the Mission of Humanity

In the aftermath of the great flood, Genesis 10 offers another genealogy. This genealogy describes the spread of humanity across the globe. Humanity appears to prosper in the post-flood world. The families of Noah's three sons spread out over the earth. The careful reader recognizes this as good news. God had originally commissioned humanity to serve as his visible representatives and to fill the earth. God's intentions for his creation include having men and women living all over the earth as witnesses to his work and character. Genesis 10:32 records that humanity is in fact spread out across the planet. Is this finally good news? Sadly, we soon discover the reason for this reality. Humanity now inhabits the entire planet, but God's mission remains incomplete. Humanity did not move across the globe with any sense of God-inspired vocation. Instead God scattered them against their will following an episode on the plains of Shinar at a place called Babel (11:1–9).

## Babel

Human rebellion and sin reemerges in 11:1–9. Humanity did not obediently move out to fill the earth, as 10:1–32 seemed to suggest. The scattering of humanity was the result of judgment by God. Genesis 11:4 is the key passage, "Come, let us build ourselves a city, with a tower that reaches to the heavens, so that we may make a name for ourselves; otherwise we will be scattered over the face of the whole earth." Humanity initiates actions that move against God's desires for humanity (cf. 1:26–31). God made a clear separation between the heavens and the earth at creation and also placed humanity on the earth as its stewards. Humanity's mission was to represent God before creation and to serve creation by building on the very goodness of its foundations. Humanity was to fulfill its mission in part by spreading out across the globe so that there would be images of the invisible and holy God everywhere. Thus, gathering on the plains of Shinar in resistance to filling the earth already represents rebellion. Humanity compounds this affront to God's mission by attempting to erect a tower to the heavens. This represents another clear challenge to the

God-desired limits on humanity. Moreover, their desire to make a name for themselves is self-serving and stands in contrast to the one name (the LORD) to which humanity may call (4:26). Humanity was created for relationship with God and to serve as God's missional community for the sake of all creation. The desire to gain power and to resist scattering is an explicit attempt to thwart God's intentions for humanity to populate the earth and serve as God's ambassadors.

Ironically, our narrative describes God's action as going down to see what the humans are up to. No matter the human capacity for ingenuity and creativity, humanity is still part of the creation and is finite in its abilities. God alone is transcendent and set apart from creation. Men and women may attempt to live as though they are sovereign. People may try to push the God-imposed boundaries. But, nevertheless, God alone reigns and freely interacts in his creation with his creatures. Against this reality, it is profound that the transcendent Creator God chooses to interact freely in our world.

The tower of Babel is not the story of individuals acting alone. It is vital to reflect on the *communal* dimension. Babel is the story of humanity conspiring as a community to accomplish a new mission. If Genesis 1:26–31 describes the original creation of humanity as the creation of a missional community that reflects God's character in/to/for the world, then 11:1–9 portrays the opposite— a community acting apart from its Creator to serve on a mission counter to God's and reflecting a self-centered, self-exalting ideology.

## Scattering and Confusion

What is God to do? Time and time again in Genesis 3–11, humanity goes its own way and thwarts God's purposes for creation. God has already hit the reset button with the great flood. He then promised to never again destroy the earth. Remarkably, in terms of Genesis 1–11, God has achieved part of his creational intentions. Due to his scattering of humanity following Babel, there are now women and men bearing God's image across the globe. But there is a profound problem—they are in no way reflecting his character and instead are demonstrating a penchant for mischief of history-altering proportions.

Chapter 11:10–26 ends with more genealogy. It traces the lineage of Noah's son Shem down to the birth of Terah's three sons: Abram, Nahor, and Haran. There is nothing remarkable here. We have already moved through multiple genealogies. We have already had our hopes dashed. After Babel, it is difficult to imagine a way forward. Fortunately the missional God is already up to something. Abram is the tenth generation from Noah just as Noah had been the tenth generation from Adam. Will Abram prove to be a new hope for humanity? Stay tuned.

## Questions for Reflection

How does God advance his mission despite the rebelliousness of humanity at Babel?

_____

_____

Reflect on the actions of humanity in Genesis 3–11. How do they describe the cause of sin?

_____

_____

What would it take for us to break out of these negative patterns and practice faithfulness in our day?

_____

_____

# Paradise Lost

## CORE TRUTHS

1. Sin and human brokenness result from our inability to trust that God has our best interests in his heart.
2. Sin damages our relationships with God, other people, and creation.
3. Sin infests and infects all people, relationships, institutions, and creation itself.
4. Despite the sinfulness of humanity and the corruption of creation's original goodness, God acts to save a remnant of humanity (Noah and his family) and issues a promise that guarantees the future of God's creation.
5. By the end of Genesis 11, God's mission reaches a watershed moment as a lost humanity has filled the earth and stands in desperate need of salvation.

## OPEN SESSION WITH PRAYER

Welcome the group and give new participants the opportunity to introduce themselves.

## DEBRIEF THE READING FOR THE WEEK (15 MINUTES)

- What were the key takeaways that you gained from this week's reading?
- What aspects of the reading did you find confusing?
- How does sin affect the world as God originally created it?
- How does God's mission change as a result of sin?

## WATCH VIDEO (30 MINUTES)

## CONVERSATION (15 MINUTES)

- What aspects of the video resonated with you most deeply?
- What questions did Brian's talk raise for you?
- How is God's response to human brokenness good news for us?
- What does Genesis 3–11 teach us about God's mission?
- Do you trust that God has your best interests at heart as well as those of whom you love the most?
- What would it take for us to break out of negative patterns of sin, injustice, and violence?
- How would your life be different if it reflected the world of Genesis 1–2 rather than the world of Genesis 3–11?
- How can we begin to live out a life in alignment with Jesus' kingdom as a witness to the world of a better way of life?

## CLOSING PRAYER

## CHAPTER FOUR

# Israel as God's New Humanity for the World

In Genesis 12–50, the LORD calls a new people into existence to serve as a new humanity through whom he will bless all people on the earth. In response to the sinfulness and corruption of Genesis 3–11, God commissions and sends a people of promise to live in the land of Canaan. The remainder of Genesis focuses on the initial generations of God's people: Abraham, Isaac, Jacob, and Jacob's twelve sons. God makes bold promises and proves his faithfulness and trustworthiness by sustaining his new people as they establish a foothold for the advance of the gospel.

# DAY 1

# God Calls Abraham

### Read Genesis 11:27–12:9

*The LORD had said to Abram, "Go from your country, your people and your
father's household to the land I will show you. I will make you into a great
nation, and I will bless you; I will make your name great, and you will be a
blessing. I will bless those who bless you, and whoever curses you I will curse;
and all peoples on earth will be blessed through you." So Abram went, as the
LORD had told him; and Lot went with him. Abram was seventy-five years
old when he set out from Harran. He took his wife Sarai, his nephew Lot,
all the possessions they had accumulated and the people they had acquired
in Harran, and they set out for the land of Canaan, and they arrived
there. Abram traveled through the land as far as the site of the great tree of
Moreh at Shechem. At that time the Canaanites were in the land. The LORD
appeared to Abram and said, "To your offspring I will give this land." So he
built an altar there to the LORD, who had appeared to him.—Genesis 12:1–7*

---

**Core Truth:** In response to the problem of a lost humanity and a
fractured creation (Genesis 3–11), God calls Abraham and his family
to live as a new humanity through whom God will bless all people.

---

After Babel, God's mission reached a pivotal moment. Humanity created
in God's image now filled the earth as God desired, but humanity is lost
and broken.

In response, God calls one family to be a new beginning for humanity and
all creation. In Genesis 12:1–3, God calls Abram (later Abraham) to a new life
for the sake of God's mission. The gospel begins here and will climax in the life,
death, and resurrection of Jesus.

## Foreshadowing Hope

God's calling of Abraham is not the first sign of his desire to restore creation. In the chaos of Genesis 3–11, God's grace was as predictable as was humanity's unfaithfulness. God sought out Adam and Eve and even covered up their nakedness. God exhorted Cain to forsake his wicked intentions. Then, even after Cain killed Abel, God protected Cain from other people. God delivered Enoch from death. God saved Noah's family and the animal kingdom from the flood. God's scattering of humanity post-Babel was a sign of his desire to continue to pursue his mission through people.

But Abraham's call is a decisive moment. Abraham and his descendants begin an unbroken line that leads to Jesus' birth and proclamation of the kingdom of God.

## Abraham's Backstory

In the aftermath of Babel, we encounter genealogies of Abraham's ancestors (11:10–32). Genesis 11:27–32 introduces the characters and the context of Abraham's call. Abraham has a wife Sarai (later Sarah). Sarah and Abraham are childless. Moreover, we discover that Abraham's father had initiated a move from Ur to the land of Canaan (modern Israel/Palestine). The family did not reach Canaan, but settled in Harran. These details provide two pieces of data: 1) God calls a person who was already on the move; 2) God calls a childless couple to become the source of blessing for the nations.

## Abraham's Call

### From the Fringes

In Genesis 12:1–3, God calls Abraham. God calls him from the old land to a new one. He grew up in Ur, a major city with ancient roots. In Abraham's time, the power centers were located in southern Mesopotamia and Egypt. But God's mission does not depend on human power. God does not save humanity by beginning in a *human* center of power. Instead, God calls a new humanity *out of* the epicenters of the day to new beginnings on the *fringes*. Canaan was inhabited, but it was more of a backwoods area. God calls Abraham to a new beginning apart from his ancestral roots. God calls him out of the world of Genesis 3–11 so that he can serve as a new humanity for the sake of the world.

## Community

We often celebrate the hero who overcomes great odds. Heroes, however, rarely act alone. Abraham is no different. God calls him, but God also calls his household (12:5). Abraham's household includes his wife, Sarah; his nephew Lot and his family; and a large extended household of servants and workers. (In Genesis 14:14, Abraham commands 318 men of fighting age.) Thus, his migration to Canaan involves an entire community. When God calls Abraham, he is calling a *community* into his mission.

## God's Promises

God makes Abraham a series of promises. These provide him assurances of success and a clear mission. God promises to make him (a childless father) into a great nation. God will bless him so that he can bless others. *To be blessed by God as a means of blessing others* is central for understanding God's mission. God's people exist for the world and not vice versa. God's call of Abraham advances God's big vision to bless all peoples. God promises security to Abraham by declaring God's intention to bless those who bless Abraham and curse those who curse him (2:2). The world is ripe with possibilities but there are also dangers. Canaan is the Promised Land, but Abraham will be in a precarious position because he will be the outsider and stranger there. God's mission is secure because God makes a series of promises to guarantee it.

## Mission

In Genesis 12:3, God tells Abraham that all families on earth will be blessed through him. This blessing is critical for understanding the missional intent of the Bible. God's people exist to extend his blessings to the nations. This is important to remember as we read the Old Testament. The Old Testament remains set within the history of the ancient world, but its narrative focuses on this new people. Outsiders only figure into the stories of the Old Testament as they encounter God's people. But this does not mean that God doesn't care about the nation. He does. God focuses on his people because he plans to use them to bless the nations. The calling of Abraham is simply the beginning of the narrative of his plan to redeem the lost world of Genesis 3–11 through a missional community. The life, death, and resurrection of Jesus will be the climax of this story.

## Abraham Goes

God has called Abraham and made promises. Will he ignore God's word like Adam, Eve, and Cain or embrace it like Noah? Genesis 12:4 captures Abram's response: "*So Abram went, as the LORD had told him.*" God's promises demonstrate that the mission depends on God's power and purposes, but God chooses to work through people.

After he arrives in Canaan, God promises the land to Abraham and his descendants (12:7). This sets the stage for the unveiling of God's kingdom. It begins with a small foothold between the powers of Egypt and Mesopotamia. This plot of land will be the setting for much of the Old Testament, for Jesus' life, and for the church's beginning. God's kingdom will transcend geography, but it begins in Canaan. God's answer to the problems of Genesis 3–11 is the calling of a missional community to reflect his character to the nations.

## Questions for Reflection

How does God's call of Abraham answer the problem of human sin narrated in Genesis 3–11?

_____

_____

How would your life need to change in order to live as an instrument of blessing to others?

_____

_____

Who is God calling you to bless today?

_____

_____

# DAY 2

# God's Faithfulness
# to His Promises

Read Genesis 18:18; 22:17–18; 26:3–5; 28:13–14

*Abraham will surely become a great and powerful nation, and all
nations on earth will be blessed through him.—Genesis 18:18*

*"Stay in this land for a while, and I will be with you and will bless you. For
to you and your descendants I will give all these lands and will confirm
the oath I swore to your father Abraham. I will make your descendants
as numerous as the stars in the sky and will give them all these lands,
and through your offspring all nations on earth will be blessed, because
Abraham obeyed me and did everything I required of him, keeping
my commands, my decrees and my instructions."—Genesis 26:3–5*

---

**Core Truth:** God's promises to Abraham, Isaac, and Jacob advance
God's mission by demonstrating his faithfulness and trustworthiness.

---

In Genesis 12–50, God demonstrates his faithfulness to Abraham and his
descendants by keeping his promises. Genesis 12–50 contains memorable
stories that testify to the faithfulness of God. God's mission advances through
his commitment to a new humanity.

God's promises to Abraham are the driving force in Genesis 12–50. The
narratives that follow Abraham's call trace how the promises of God pass from
generation to generation. God appears to Isaac and Jacob to reaffirm his earlier
promises to Abraham.

The theme of promise demonstrates the faithfulness of God despite the
missteps of Israel's ancestors. God is faithful when Abraham, Isaac, and Jacob

are faithful, but God is faithful even when they are not. God's people have ethical responsibilities, but Genesis 12–50 offers an alternative to the narratives of Genesis 3–11 where humanity was lost in perpetual cycles of sin and disobedience. Genesis 12–50 stresses that God's mission advances through the faithfulness of God. Humanity has a role, but Scripture grounds the success of God's mission in only one place—God himself.

## Abraham, Isaac, and the Promise

God keeps his promises. God sustains the community of Abraham, Isaac, and Jacob despite threats to God's promises. These threats were usually the result of the failings of God's people. When Abraham twice passes off Sarah as his sister (see Gen. 12:10–20 and 20:1–18), Pharaoh and later Abimelek take her as a wife. God intervenes each time to restore Sarah to Abraham. God called Sarah to be the mother of a people of promise so he protected her. In Genesis 16, Abraham has a son (Ishmael) through Sarah's slave-girl, Hagar, who serves as a surrogate. This was an accepted cultural practice, but it was not God's plan. Ishmael was Abraham's firstborn, but he was not the promised son. The promised son would come directly from the union of Sarah and Abraham. Sarah gives birth to Isaac through the power of God. Ishmael receives a special blessing (21:17–18), but it is Isaac whom God choses to serve as the promise bearer (26:3–4). In the next generation, Isaac mirrors the actions of Abraham by passing off his wife, Rebekah, as his sister (26:7–10).

## Jacob and the Promise

Jacob is the greatest example of God's faithfulness despite the brokenness of his people. Though second born to Esau, Jacob is God's choice while still in the womb (25:23), but Jacob proves to be an unethical manipulator of events and people. He gains Esau's birthright by taking advantage of Esau's hunger. He plots with his mother, Rebekah, to deceive Isaac into granting Jacob the blessing of the firstborn (Gen. 27–28). Then, due to Esau's understandable anger, Jacob has to flee for his life to Haran and leave the Promised Land of Canaan. At this moment, Jacob encounters God for the first time. In Genesis 28:13–15, God passes on to Jacob his earlier promises to Abraham and Isaac. This encounter does not change Jacob. While in Haran, Jacob works to outwit his uncle Laban and accumulates vast wealth (29–31). Jacob again has to flee. While fretting over the necessity of meeting up with Esau again, Jacob encounters God at the river Jabbok. He wrestles with God. During this encounter, God blesses Jacob and gives him the name Israel. This encounter transforms Jacob as he finally relinquishes self-control and recognizes his need for God. The next day when Jacob encounters Esau, Esau forgives Jacob and welcomes his brother home. God's faithfulness overcomes Jacob's deceitfulness. In fact, Israel (Jacob) has twelve sons whose descendants become the twelve tribes of Israel. His favorite of his twelve sons, Joseph, is despised by his brothers and sold into slavery.

## Joseph and God's Faithfulness

Joseph's story (Gen. 37–50) centers on the ongoing providential care that God gives to his new humanity. In these chapters, God guides Joseph through the slavery brought on by the jealousy of his brothers, to imprisonment in Egypt, to rising as Pharaoh's second in command. Joseph remains unbroken and God works through him to bless others. While in prison, Joseph interprets dreams. This leads to the miraculous series of events that leads him to interpret Pharaoh's dream. When Pharaoh hears Joseph's interpretation, he recognizes God's presence in Joseph's life (41:38). He then appoints Joseph as his second in command and Joseph leads Egypt to prepare successfully for a famine. The famine also affects Canaan, where his father, Jacob, and his family still live. Jacob sends his sons to Egypt to purchase food. In a remarkable story, Joseph reconciles with his brothers who had sold him into slavery. Pharaoh invites Joseph's entire family to live in Egypt as his guests. In the rest of Genesis, God's people live in Egypt as Pharaoh's guests.

In Genesis 45:4–8 and 50:19–21, Joseph assures his brothers that there will be no retaliation against them. Genesis 50:20 is profound, "You intended to harm me, but God intended it for good to accomplish what is now being done, the saving of many lives." God intends and works *good* regardless of the circumstances in which God's people find themselves. This does not mean that God's people will avoid suffering. Hardships are the reality of living in the post-fall world. But God faithfully advances his mission and keeps his promises. Joseph embodies faithfulness in light of God's promises. Joseph is able to understand the circumstances and challenges of his own life in light of God's promises and mission. At the end of his life (Gen. 50:22–26), Joseph takes up the mantle of Abraham, Isaac, and Jacob by affirming to his brothers that God will indeed lead the people back to the Promised Land of Canaan.

Genesis 12–50 exhorts God's people to recognize their standing in the world as a people of promise. God's people exist as a missional community for the sake of the world. God's faithfulness to his promises assures a good future. God's relentless faithfulness ought to embolden his people to faithful living in whatever circumstances they find themselves.

## Questions for Reflection

How is it important for your own faith to know that God keeps his promises?

_____

_____

What role do God's faithfulness and the faithfulness of God's people play in the advance of God's mission in Genesis 12–50?

_____

_____

# DAY 3

# Holiness and God's Promises

Genesis 17:1–14; 22:1–18

*Isaac spoke up and said to his father Abraham, "Father?" "Yes, my son?" Abraham replied. "The fire and wood are here," Isaac said, "but where is the lamb for the burnt offering?" Abraham answered, "God himself will provide the lamb for the burnt offering, my son." And the two of them went on together. When they reached the place God had told him about, Abraham built an altar there and arranged the wood on it. He bound his son Isaac and laid him on the altar, on top of the wood. Then he reached out his hand and took the knife to slay his son. But the angel of the LORD called out to him from heaven, "Abraham! Abraham!" "Here I am," he replied. "Do not lay a hand on the boy," he said. "Do not do anything to him. Now I know that you fear God, because you have not withheld from me your son, your only son." Abraham looked up and there in a thicket he saw a ram caught by its horns. He went over and took the ram and sacrificed it as a burnt offering instead of his son. So Abraham called that place The LORD Will Provide. And to this day it is said, "On the mountain of the LORD it will be provided."—Genesis 22:7–14*

---

**Core Truth:** Faithful obedience enhances the missional success of the people of God.

---

God's people are a missional community that reflects God's character in/to/ for the world. Genesis 12–50 is fundamentally about God's faithfulness in the progress of his mission to bring blessing to the world through Abraham and his family. How does the character of God's people fit into this?

## Abraham and Holiness

In Genesis 17, God establishes a covenant with Abraham, including the ritual of circumcision as its sign. This is the second covenant in the Old Testament after God's covenant with Noah and all creation (Gen. 9:1–17). In Genesis 17, God promises Abraham's descendants, but it includes the expectation of faithfulness on the part of Abraham. Genesis 17:1–2 reads: "I am God Almighty; walk before me faithfully and be blameless. Then I will make my covenant between me and you and will greatly increase your numbers." In Genesis 17, God gives him the new name "Abraham" to memorialize this key point in his life.[7] These opening verses announce the expectation of a lifestyle in line with God's character. Earlier the words "walk" and "blameless" described Noah (6:9) and Enoch (5:24). Genesis 17 does not describe the faithful life other than the necessity of circumcision for all males within the community. God does not reveal the specifics of faithfulness until God gives his law at Sinai (see Exod. 19:1–Num. 10:10 and the book of Deuteronomy).

Genesis 18:18–19 echoes the expectation of faithfulness:

> "Abraham will surely become a great and powerful nation, and all nations on earth will be blessed through him. For I have chosen him, so that he will direct his children and his household after him to keep the way of the LORD by doing what is right and just, so that the LORD will bring about for Abraham what he has promised him."

In Genesis 18, God is poised to destroy Sodom and Gomorrah because of the wickedness found in those cities. God reveals his intentions to Abraham. In response, Abraham intercedes successfully on behalf of his nephew Lot (18:22–33). With the negative example of the wickedness of Sodom and Gomorrah in the immediate context, verses 18–19 clearly present a contrast between God's expectations for Abraham and the lifestyle/ethos of Sodom and Gomorrah. They establish an expectation that Abraham will *direct* his children in God's way. In this context we clearly see all three elements of GPS—(G)od's mission, (P)ersons in Community, and (S)pirit-transformed. Abraham's family (community) was to embody a distinct ethos (holiness) as part of embodying the promise of serving as a blessing for all nations (mission).

## Abraham and Obedience

The ultimate test of Abraham's obedience comes with God's request that he sacrifice his promised son, Isaac (Gen. 22). The thought of God asking someone to sacrifice a child is disturbing, but such sacrifices were not unusual in the ancient world. The Bible focuses on the reality that God provides a ram in the place of Isaac. Genesis 22 is climactic in the Abrahamic story and demonstrates both Abraham's and God's faithfulness. In light of the life, death, and resurrection of Jesus, Genesis 22 anticipates God doing precisely what he did not ask of Abraham. God, through the person of God's son, Jesus of Nazareth, dies so that all may live.

God speaks these words to Abraham:

> "I swear by myself, declares the LORD, that because you have done this and have not withheld your son, your only son, I will surely bless you and make your descendants as numerous as the stars in the sky and as the sand on the seashore. Your descendants will take possession of the cities of their enemies, and through your offspring all nations on earth will be blessed, because you have obeyed me." (Gen. 22:16–18)

Abraham's willingness to follow God's command to sacrifice Isaac epitomizes faithful obedience. This text embodies the tension between God's unconditional promises and the necessity of human response. We need to read God's words to Abraham as an affirmation of his *faithful obedience*. God had already promised Abraham these things. Abraham's obedience was not the cause of the God's promises, but Abraham's obedience points the way forward for God's people. It is the desired response to God's prior grace.

## Isaac and Holiness

In Genesis 26:2–5, God extends to Isaac the promises initiated with Abraham. God appears during a time of famine and assures Isaac of his presence with him lest Isaac flee to Egypt. Verse five is critical for our reflection on the ethics of Israel's ancestors. God cites Abraham's obedience as the basis for renewing the promises for Isaac. God promises Isaac land, many descendants, and the mission of blessing the nations. Abraham's willingness to listen to God's voice functions as a model for Isaac. Obedience enhances the ability of God's people to advance his mission in the world.

## Joseph's Faithfulness

In Genesis 39, Joseph models faithful obedience in difficult circumstances. Joseph is serving as a slave in Egypt in the household of Potiphar, an officer under the Egyptian pharaoh. The handsome Joseph attracts the sexual advances of Potiphar's wife. Joseph resists her by asserting his faithfulness in serving Potiphar and in verse 9 he adds, "How then could I do such a wicked thing and sin against God?" Joseph is motivated by his desire to serve faithfully as a witness to God. He will not act in ways that dishonor God. This is the essence of missional holiness. Joseph understands that his actions directly impact the way that others would perceive his god.

## Missional Holiness

Holiness matters. Faithful obedience enhances the missional success of the people of God. Too much is at stake in God's mission to disregard this aspect. God's call of Abraham and his descendants is certainly an unconditional offer of promise and blessing. God does offer unmerited grace and promises to Abraham, Isaac, and Jacob, yet these unconditional blessings nonetheless require a human response. Genesis 12–50 is more interested in demonstrating the grace and faithfulness of the LORD, but the need for a holy community is present. The books of Exodus through Deuteronomy will explore this theme in more depth.

## Questions for Reflection

What is your understanding of the relationship between God's unconditional promises and our response of faithful living?

_____

_____

How does faithful living enhance God's mission?

_____

_____

To what god or cause does your life point? How would your life be different if you realigned with the God of the Bible today?

_____

_____

# DAY 4

# Privilege, Power, and the Mission of God

### Read Genesis 21:1–21; Psalm 113

*Now the LORD was gracious to Sarah as he had said, and the LORD did for Sarah what he had promised. Sarah became pregnant and bore a son to Abraham in his old age, at the very time God had promised him. Abraham gave the name Isaac to the son Sarah bore him. When his son Isaac was eight days old, Abraham circumcised him, as God commanded him. Abraham was a hundred years old when his son Isaac was born to him. Sarah said, "God has brought me laughter, and everyone who hears about this will laugh with me." And she added, "Who would have said to Abraham that Sarah would nurse children? Yet I have borne him a son in his old age."—Genesis 21:1-7*

---

**Core Truth:** The advance of God's mission does not depend on traditional human power structures or practices.

---

God consistently, relentlessly, and faithfully keeps his promises to his people in Genesis 12–50. These chapters use the themes of childlessness and the reversal of the firstborn's privilege to teach us key truths about God and God's mission.

## Blessing the Childless

Childlessness recurs throughout Genesis 12–50. It affects Abraham/Sarah and Isaac/Rebekah. Childlessness functions to mark God's people as the product of his grace and not human power. God calls Abraham and Sarah to be the wellspring for a new humanity that exists for the sake of the nations. Abraham obeys and trusts God, but he has no son. God renews his promises to Abraham in 15:1–6. His trust in God is reckoned as righteousness (15:6), but there is still no son. In chapter 16, Abraham and Sarah take matters into their own hands by conceiving a child through Sarah's slave, Hagar. This was an acceptable practice, but God planned a miraculous birth. Childlessness is no obstacle for God. Thus, late in life and according to God's promise (18:10), Sarah bears a son named Isaac. Isaac and Rebekah face the same challenge. God opens Rebekah's womb in response to Isaac's petition, and she gives birth to twins: Esau and Jacob.

God's ability to bless the childless recurs throughout the Old Testament. In Psalm 113, the psalmist declares God's care and compassion for the marginalized. Verse 9 announces, "[the Lord] settles the childless woman in her home as a happy mother of children. Praise the LORD."

Likewise, Isaiah (54:1) proclaims, "'Sing, barren woman, you who never bore a child; burst into song, shout for joy, you who were never in labor; because more are the children of the desolate woman than of her who has a husband,' says the LORD." Isaiah speaks these words as a means of encouraging those waiting for God's salvation.

What is the point of this theme? God's salvation is not dependent on human power or ability. God's mission depends on God's strength and power. God demonstrates this by multiplying descendants for Abraham through couples unable to bear children. It also reminds us that God works through people whom many communities marginalize.

## Reversal of the Privilege of the Firstborn

In Genesis 12–50, Isaac supplants Ishmael, Jacob gains the elder Esau's birthright, and Joseph rules over his family. The firstborn son carried a position of power in the ancient world. This was a means of insuring the success and prestige of the family by investing the family's resources in the firstborn. God does not need the status quo power structures of humanity to advance his mission. God works through the powerless, the humble, and the overlooked. This means that God often bypassed the firstborn in favor of a younger son. We saw this first in the Cain and Abel story.

In Abraham's narrative, Ishmael is his firstborn. Abraham beget Ishmael with his own strength, but God intended something greater. In Genesis 18,

God renews his promise that Sarah will bear a child (18:10). Abraham and Sarah were well beyond the normal child-bearing years. God keeps his word and Genesis 21:1–7 records the birth of Isaac. Abraham is one hundred years old at Isaac's birth. Ishmael was approximately fourteen years old. There is instant tension between Sarah/Isaac and Hagar/Ishmael. Sarah demands that Abraham expel Hagar whom she refers to as "that slave woman" and Ishmael whom Sarah calls "[Hagar's] son" (21:10). The expulsion of Hagar and Ishmael is tragic from a relational perspective, but God steps in to redeem it. Ishmael is a son of Abraham after all. God's blessing extends to those in proximity to Abraham as well, so in 21:13 God affirms that Ishmael will indeed become a "great nation" too. Genesis 25:12–18 records the fulfillment of this promise. Ishmael becomes the father of twelve sons who become princes of a twelve-tribe confederation analogous to the line of Abraham, Isaac, and Jacob.

The rivalry between Esau and Jacob begins at conception (25:33). At birth, Esau arrives first with Jacob hanging onto his heel. But Rebekah already knows that God has ordained the elder to serve the younger. In God's plan, it will be Jacob and not Esau through whom the lineage of God's people will continue. This choice does not depend on Jacob's character in any way. Jacob is deceitful and a rogue. God's choice of Jacob does not render Esau's life meaningless or a failure. Esau remains linked to the family of blessing and thus is blessed. He accumulates wealth for himself (33:9) and becomes the father of the Edomites (36:40).

Lastly, the rivalry between Joseph and his brothers dominates Genesis 37–50. Joseph is the eleventh of twelve sons. Yet Jacob favors him because he was the firstborn son of his beloved wife, Rachel. This causes tension and jealousy within the family and his brothers sell him into slavery. Joseph ends up in Egypt where God prospers him. After Joseph interprets the dream of Pharaoh, he elevates Joseph from imprisoned slave to a leadership role second only to himself. God's providential care for his people is evident in Joseph's extraordinary story. Joseph rises to power precisely in time to create a safe haven in Egypt so that God's people can persevere and grow during a period of severe famine.

In all of these stories, God demonstrates his power to save by working through a younger son rather than the firstborn. This subverts a claim to human power in the advance of the gospel.

## Conclusion

God's mission moves forward by his grace. God makes and keeps promises. God overcomes broken family relationships, ill intentions, and even human infertility to advance the family through whom the nations will be blessed (Gen. 12:3b). God's people grow from a childless couple to a substantial presence in Egypt. God reverses cultural bias toward the firstborn to advance his kingdom. Genesis 3–11 demonstrates humanity's inability to find its own way and its penchant for spectacular failure. The stories of Abraham, Isaac, and Jacob point to a new hope. This hope finds its roots in God's faithfulness and commitment to his people. The themes of childlessness and the flipping of the privileged role of firstborn serve to proclaim this.

## Questions for Reflection

How do God's actions toward the marginalized and powerless encourage you?

_____

_____

How would you live your life differently if you truly believed that your future could be empowered by God rather than limited by human traditions and power structures?

_____

_____

# DAY 5

# Abraham and the Gospel

Read Matthew 1:1; Romans 4:1–25; Galatians 3–4;
James 2:14–24

*This is the genealogy of Jesus the Messiah the son of
David, the son of Abraham.—Matthew 1:1*

---

**Core Truth:** The New Testament uses Abraham as an example of the central role of faith in a person's life and as a model of faithfully living in ways that reflect God's character.

---

In the New Testament, Abraham plays a critical role. The New Testament writers deploy Abraham's legacy to proclaim the gospel of Jesus.

## The Gospel of Matthew

Matthew begins with Jesus' genealogy (1:1–17). Son of Abraham is one of three titles for Jesus in Matthew 1:1 (Son of Abraham, Son of David, Messiah). Matthew begins with Abraham because he links Jesus to the nations of Genesis 1–11. As the son of Abraham, Jesus will open the kingdom to both Jews and Gentiles. Jesus will be the son of Abraham through whom all peoples will be blessed.

In Matthew 8:5–13, Jesus heals the servant of a Roman centurion. Jesus, moved by the centurion's faith, says, "Truly I tell you, I have not found anyone in Israel with such great faith" (8:10). He remarks that people will come from all parts of the globe to feast with Abraham, whereas prior subjects of the kingdom will find themselves excluded from the feast. This is a warning to believers to stay connected with God's missional goals and recognize that many "outsiders" who are seeking after God will find themselves on the inside.

# The Apostle Paul

*Romans 4:1–25*

In his writings, Paul uses Abraham to model faith and as a forerunner of the gospel. Paul writes to the Roman believers to introduce himself and articulate his understanding of the gospel in advance of his visit to Rome. Paul writes about a key question for the early church: Do Christians have to follow the Law of Moses? This was an identity question. Do Christ-followers experience the righteousness of God through faith in Christ or through the practice of covenant acts such as dietary law, circumcision, or Sabbath keeping? Paul is adamant that righteousness is by faith. He points to Abraham as the fore-runner of the good news. Paul finds in Abraham the model for the life of faith. Paul quotes Genesis 15:6, "Abram believed the LORD, and he credited it to him as righteousness." Abraham related to God through faith rather than through works of the Law. Abraham's position in Israel's story is significant because Abraham predates the Law of Moses. Paul is not declaring the Law worthless or misguided. He affirms that people connect with God through faith. The Law of Moses is not the basis for salvation but means by which God's people respond to grace (see more on this in chapter 6).

*Galatians 3–4*

Galatians is Paul's most argumentative letter. The churches of Galatia are divided over the nature of the gospel. Do male converts to Christianity need to be circumcised as a male convert to Judaism had to be? One faction argued for the necessity of adopting Jewish practices rooted in the Law of Moses as foundational for the Christian life. Paul sees this as a threat to the gospel and deploys Abraham's legacy as a rebuttal.

In Galatians 3:1–14, Paul centers the gospel on faith in Jesus Christ as the basis for our acceptance by God. Salvation is a gift of God through faith and not something attained through works of the Law. As in Romans, Paul cites Abraham as the father of faith (3:6). Gentiles and Jews alike demonstrate that they are children of Abraham by trusting God. Paul then quotes Genesis 12:3, "All the Gentiles shall be blessed in you" (Gal. 3:8) to show that God announced the gospel in advance to Abraham regarding how Gentiles would be included in God's people.

In 3:15–22, Paul declares that Jesus is the fulfillment of God's promises to Abraham and his seed/offspring (cf. Gen. 12:7). God made promises that his people receive through grace rather than works. Believers today receive the promises of God through faith in Jesus.

In 4:21–31, Paul uses Abraham's two sons, Isaac and Ishmael, and their mothers, Sarah and Hagar, to contrast faith with works of the law. The struggle between Isaac/Sarah and Ishmael/Hagar becomes an allegory to teach us the gospel. They represent two different types of children for Abraham: free and slave. Paul declares that it will not be the Gentiles who end up slave children but those who embrace works rather than faith. Ishmael/Hagar represent a covenant of slavery rooted in human effort and centered in Jerusalem (this is Paul's depiction of how his opponents in Galatia understood the law). In contrast, Isaac/Sarah represent the new movement of the Spirit of the heavenly Jerusalem that manifests itself in the gospel of freedom. Paul reminds his readers that only the child of the free woman will receive the inheritance.

## James 2:14–24

James addresses a different situation than the ones faced by Paul. James articulates a Christian way of life for his mainly Jewish-Christian audience. Ethical living is the natural expression of the faithful life. James's church is failing to practice kindness and charity to fellow believers. Rich believers are receiving privileges and honor at the expense of the poor. James reminds them that Abraham demonstrated his allegiance to God through how he lived. Unlike Paul, James is not writing about acceptance by God. James exhorts his audience to live out their faith moment by moment. Holy living is the natural expression of faith in Jesus. Abraham, in the near sacrifice of Isaac, demonstrated his commitment to God. Like Paul, James quotes from Genesis 15:6 (2:23), but emphasizes that faith must manifest itself moment by moment in faithfulness.

Abraham's influence extends into the New Testament. Abraham witnesses to the primacy of faith in Christ and shows that faith *must* be lived out in ways that truly reflect God's character.

## Questions for Reflection

How does Abraham serve as a model for faith?

_____

_____

How does the New Testament's use of Abraham show the importance of the Old Testament in telling the story of Jesus?

_____

_____

What would your life look like if the Bible's story became your story?

_____

_____

# Israel as God's New Humanity for the World

## CORE TRUTHS

1. In response to the problem of a lost humanity and a fractured creation (Genesis 3–11), God calls Abraham and his family to live as a new humanity through whom God will bless all people.
2. God's promises to Abraham, Isaac, and Jacob advance God's mission by demonstrating his faithfulness and trustworthiness.
3. Faithful obedience enhances the missional success of the people of God.
4. The advance of God's mission does not depend on traditional human power structures or practices.
5. The New Testament uses Abraham as an example of the central role of faith in a person's life and as a model of faithfully living in ways that reflect God's character.

## OPEN SESSION WITH PRAYER

Welcome the group and give new participants the opportunity to introduce themselves.

## DEBRIEF THE READING FOR THE WEEK (15 MINUTES)

- What were the key takeaways that you gained from this week's reading?
- What aspects of the reading did you find confusing?
- How does God's call of Abraham answer the problem of human sin narrated in Genesis 3–11?

- What does Genesis 12–50 teach us about God?
- What role do God's promises play in Genesis 12–50?

## WATCH VIDEO (30 MINUTES)

## CONVERSATION (15 MINUTES)

- What aspects of the message resonated with you most deeply?
- What questions did Brian's talk raise for you?
- Who can God bless through your life?
- What role does faithfulness play in the life of faith?
- What is your understanding of the relationship between God's unconditional promises and our response of faithful living?
- How would you live your life differently if you truly believed that your future could be empowered by God rather than limited by human traditions and power structures?

## CLOSING PRAYER

## CHAPTER FIVE

# Exodus, Liberation, and the Mission of God

Genesis sets the stage for understanding the Bible as the story of God's mission. The four books that follow (Exodus, Leviticus, Numbers, and Deuteronomy) accelerate it. In the next two chapters, we will explore key themes that emerge from these books. The five books (Genesis–Deuteronomy) are often referred to as the Pentateuch, or the Law.

In the book of Exodus, God delivers God's people from slavery in Egypt in order to serve as God's missional people for the world. God leads Israel from Egypt, guides them through the wilderness, and enters into a new covenant with his people at Sinai.

# DAY 1

# Exodus as a Foundational Event

### Read Psalms 114; 136

*Give thanks to the LORD, for he is good. "His love endures forever."
Give thanks to the God of gods. "His love endures forever." Give thanks
to the Lord of lords: "His love endures forever." to him who alone does
great wonders, "His love endures forever." who by his understanding
made the heavens, "His love endures forever." who spread out the earth
upon the waters, "His love endures forever." who made the great lights—
"His love endures forever." the sun to govern the day, "His love endures
forever." the moon and stars to govern the night; "His love endures
forever." to him who struck down the firstborn of Egypt "His love
endures forever." and brought Israel out from among them "His love
endures forever." with a mighty hand and outstretched arm; "His
love endures forever." to him who divided the Red Sea asunder "His
love endures forever." and brought Israel through the midst of it, "His
love endures forever." but swept Pharaoh and his army into the Red
Sea; "His love endures forever." to him who led his people through
the wilderness; "His love endures forever."—Psalm 136:1–16*

> **Core Truth:** The LORD saved his oppressed people from Egypt for
> the sake of his mission to bless the nations.

The book of Exodus contains three critical elements for understanding
God's work in the world and our place in it: deliverance from Egypt, covenant at Sinai, and presence with God's people.

## Exodus as the Heart of Israel's Gospel

The heart of Israel's gospel is its story of how the LORD saved his oppressed people from Egypt for the sake of his mission to bless the nations. The exodus serves as the basis for Israel's way of life as well as the foundation for its self-understanding and hope. God forges a relationship with his people through his gracious actions. The life of God's people is nothing more and nothing less than a whole-hearted response to his grace.

The Ten Commandments (Exod. 20:1–17; Deut. 5:6–21) open with the historic reminder "I am the LORD your God, who brought you out of Egypt, out of the land of slavery." Before there is law, there is God's grace that creates and makes relationship possible.

Throughout the Old Testament, Israel's praise continually remembers God's deliverance from Egypt. Here are a few examples from Psalms:

to him who struck down the firstborn of Egypt  "His love endures forever."
and brought Israel out from among them  "His love endures forever."
with a mighty hand and outstretched arm;  "His love endures forever."
(Ps. 136:10–12)

You transplanted a vine from Egypt; you drove out the nations and planted it. (Ps. 80:8)

When Israel came out of Egypt, the house of Jacob from a people of foreign tongue. (Ps. 114:1)

In the exodus, God liberates his people to serve as a missional community that reflects his character in/to/for the world. It demonstrates and proves his faithfulness and love. God's people can trust that their present and future is secure. This is good news to be shared. It announces to the world (including Egypt) a God who desires to bless all people and nations. It is a counter-cultural reminder that the LORD is not a defender of the status quo or of only the privileged and powerful. The message of Exodus provides a profound hope for all people who long for justice. The God, who created the world to be "very good" and embedded Sabbath into the fabric of life, acts in human history. God acts on behalf of justice and on behalf of his mission to bless the nations by intervening in human affairs to save the descendants of Abraham, Isaac, and Jacob whom Egypt unjustly enslaved.

## Covenant: Faithfulness in Response to Grace

The purpose of the deliverance is not simply liberation from the oppression of Egypt. Rather the ultimate purpose is dynamic relationship with God for the sake of the world. It is always good for justice to prevail. But the goal of the exodus is the freedom to serve God rather than autonomous freedom. God frees his people to unleash them for his mission to bless the nations in fulfillment of Abraham's call (Gen. 12:3). This unleashing takes place within the context of covenant. The Sinai covenant makes up the majority of Exodus–Numbers. Exodus 19:1–Numbers 10:10 narrate Israel's stay at Sinai and provide the details of the covenant. This is the third covenant in the Bible after Noah's and Abraham's. In the Sinai covenant, God calls Israel to live as a community called to bless the nations by embodying the character of God. The Sinai covenant assumes the missional nature of God's people. Israel exists as a kingdom of priests for the rest of the world, but Sinai emphasizes the creation of a holy community (Exod. 19:5–6). God's people can only achieve their mission of representing God to the nations by actually living in a way that reflects God's holy character. As we will see, this involves loving God and loving others.

## Relational Wholeness: God with Us

The book of Exodus climaxes in God's presence coming to dwell in the newly constructed tabernacle in the midst of the Israelite camp (Exod. 40:34–38). Most gods of the ancient world lived in temples on cosmic mountains. Think of Zeus on Mount Olympus or the Canaanite god Baal on Mount Zaphon. The LORD is different. God chooses to dwell with his people. God abides with and leads his people as they move toward the Promised Land in fulfillment of the promises to Abraham, Isaac, and Jacob. Unlike the gods of the nations, the LORD desires to be in relationship with humanity. In the contemporary world, most of us assume that God is on our side. This was not an assumption or worldview of the ancients. In the ancient world, the powerful gods sided with powerful people. If you were among the bottom 99 percent of the world, you lived to fear and placate the gods. The Bible offers a potent counter-narrative to this. As we've already seen, God created all men and all women in the image of God to reflect his character to the world and to care for creation. Genesis 3–11 narrates humanity's lostness and brokenness. Beginning with Abraham, God is working to reverse the tragedy of human sin and reforge the relational wholeness of creation. The tabernacle shows this by highlighting God's desire to dwell with his people at the center of their community. This is profoundly good news. With God's real presence at the center of their community, Israel becomes a missional community for the rest of the world.

## Questions for Reflection

The exodus served to secure Israel's present and future. What story currently serves to guide your life and provide you peace and security?

_____

_____

What do the themes of Exodus show you about God, his mission, and our place in it?

_____

_____

# DAY 2

# God Calls
# and Commissions Moses

Read Exodus 2:23–4:17

*When the Lord saw that he had gone over to look, God called to him
from within the bush, "Moses! Moses!" And Moses said, "Here I am."
"Do not come any closer," God said. "Take off your sandals, for the place
where you are standing is holy ground." Then he said, "I am the God
of your father, the God of Abraham, the God of Isaac and the God of
Jacob." At this, Moses hid his face, because he was afraid to look at God.
The Lord said, "I have indeed seen the misery of my people in Egypt.
I have heard them crying out because of their slave drivers, and I am
concerned about their suffering. So I have come down to rescue them from
the hand of the Egyptians and to bring them up out of that land into a
good and spacious land, a land flowing with milk and honey—the home
of the Canaanites, Hittites, Amorites, Perizzites, Hivites and Jebusites.
And now the cry of the Israelites has reached me, and I have seen the
way the Egyptians are oppressing them. So now, go. I am sending you to
Pharaoh to bring my people the Israelites out of Egypt."—Exodus 3:4–10*

---

**Core Truth:** The Lord calls, commissions, and equips Moses to serve
as his agent of deliverance.

---

God advances his mission through people. Moses is one of the giants. Moses
is born at a critical moment in history. Genesis concludes with Israel in
Egypt. Jacob's family has multiplied greatly (Exod. 1:6–7). This growth echoed
God's instructions to the first humans (Gen. 1:28; cf. Gen. 9:7). In Egypt, Israel
is fulfilling God's creational goals. God's promises to Israel's ancestors are

coming true. They are becoming a great nation (Gen. 12:1–3) as numerous as the stars (Gen. 15:5). Unfortunately, Pharaoh the king of Egypt views this as a threat to Egypt's security (Exod. 1:8–10). Pharaoh responds by enslaving the Israelites and attempting to destroy Israel through forced labor. He also orders that all male Hebrew children be killed.

## Moses' Birth and Early Years

Moses is born in the midst of this chaos (2:2). Moses' mother hides him for three months before placing him in a basket in the Nile River. The Hebrew word translated "basket" is the same word translated "ark" in Noah's story. God protects Moses from destruction just as he did Noah. Astonishingly, Pharaoh's daughter spies Moses' ark and rescues him. She adopts Moses. Israel now has a son in the royal household (2:10). Could deliverance be near?

The story takes a negative turn when the adult Moses kills an Egyptian who is beating an Israelite (2:11–15). This is the only attempt to use *pure human power* and *violence* to liberate God's people. God will deliver Israel through his power and not mere *human power*. Human violence plays no role in the deliverance from Egypt. This is a key lesson for us. God is the savior, not us.

Moses flees for his life and ends up in Midian (the modern Sinai Peninsula). Moses joins the family of Reuel/Jethro, marrying his daughter Zipporah. Moses aptly names his firstborn son, Gershom, which means "I have become a foreigner in a foreign land" (2:22). This name reminds us that Moses is a foreigner in Midian and of Israel's plight in Egypt. What has become of God's promises?

## God Arises

Exodus 2:23–25 dynamically announces God's response to the oppression in Egypt. God *heard* the cries of Israel. God *remembered* his covenant with Israel's ancestors. God *saw* and *was concerned*. Rather than suggesting God's forgetfulness, it announces that God is poised and ready to deliver Israel just as God delivered Noah from the flood (see Gen. 8:1 for a similar use of God *remembered*). God will act powerfully to make his name known and to liberate his people.

## God Calls Moses

In Exodus 3:1–4:17, Moses experiences a high-altitude encounter with God on Mount Sinai/Horeb. God speaks to him from a burning bush and calls Moses to his mission. He introduces himself to Moses: "I am the God of your father, the God of Abraham, the God of Isaac, and the God of Jacob" (3:6). He tells Moses that he has come down to rescue his people from Egypt and to bring them to the Promised Land of Canaan. Moses will serve as his agent for deliverance.

Moses hesitates, questions his identity, and expresses self-doubt over his ability (3:11). God's answer is critical for our role in mission. God promises his presence. This is enough. It is not about the one called; it is about the God who calls and promises presence. God's presence is a key theme, whose fullest expression occurs in the birth of Jesus (Immanuel "God with us" [Isa. 7:14; cf. Matt. 1:23]).

Moses then wants to know God's identity. Who is the God of Abraham? God replies mysteriously, "I AM WHO I AM" (3:14). God identifies himself as Yahweh (the LORD) explicitly for the first time in Scripture. This is a key moment. The God who delivers Israel from Egypt is the same God who created the world and called Abraham. Israel now knows that God's name is the LORD. Yet this revelation is an invitation to learn more about God. "I AM WHO I AM" can also be translated "I will be who I will be" or even "I will be who I want to be." The LORD will be known by his actions. In two later passages (Exod. 20:2 and 34:6–7), we will encounter more self-revelations of God's character.

God announces to Moses his plan (3:16–22). He promises to deliver Israel with a "mighty hand," as Pharaoh will refuse to release God's people. The looming showdown with Pharaoh will be epic.

Unsatisfied, Moses doubts his ability to persuade Israel (4:1). The LORD provides Moses with three signs that will establish his authority. These signs include the abilities to turn his hand leprous, transform a staff into a serpent, and turn water into blood. Then, Moses laments that he lacks public speaking ability (4:10). God responds by promising to empower Moses' speaking ability.

Finally, Moses' real objection comes to the surface. He asks God to send someone else (4:13). It is only at this moment that the LORD becomes angry. God has called Moses, promised his presence, shared his name, provided powerful signs, and empowered his speech. All Moses must do is *act*. This is a profound lesson: God equips those whom he calls. All God requires is our faithfulness in taking the first steps on the journey on which God sends us.

Moses finally steps forward. God sends Moses' brother Aaron to serve as Moses' mouthpiece in the mission. Moses announces his return to Egypt and leaves Midian with his family.

God still calls people today. God's call may come in various ways. But rest assured, he will equip us for the journey.

## Questions for Reflection

How does God's interaction with Moses illustrate his desire for relationships with people?

_____

_____

What talents has God given you to use for serving others?

_____

_____

How might God be calling you to serve?

_____

_____

# DAY 3

# The LORD Is King of All Creation

Read Exodus 4:21–23; 5:1–2; 9:13–10:1–2

*Afterward Moses and Aaron went to Pharaoh and said, "This is what the LORD, the God of Israel, says: 'Let my people go, so that they may hold a festival to me in the wilderness.'" Pharaoh said, "Who is the LORD, that I should obey him and let Israel go? I do not know the LORD and I will not let Israel go."—Exodus 5:1–2*

*Then the LORD said to Moses, "Get up early in the morning, confront Pharaoh and say to him, 'This is what the LORD, the God of the Hebrews, says: Let my people go, so that they may worship me, or this time I will send the full force of my plagues against you and against your officials and your people, so you may know that there is no one like me in all the earth. For by now I could have stretched out my hand and struck you and your people with a plague that would have wiped you off the earth. But I have raised you up for this very purpose, that I might show you my power and that my name might be proclaimed in all the earth.'"—Exodus 9:13–16*

> **Core Truth:** In the exodus from Egypt, God delivers his people and reveals his grace and power to save to the world.

What kingdom will we serve—God's or some other? The beginning of Exodus has set the stage for a showdown for the service of God's people. In Exodus 1, Pharaoh illegitimately enslaves God's people. Pharaoh and all of Egypt interpreted the growth of Israel as a threat rather than as a sign of God's blessing. In response, Pharaoh instituted genocidal policies to erase Israel from history. Exodus presents Pharaoh as both an oppressor and an anti-creational force that threatens God's mission to bless the nations.

## Prelude to Deliverance

En route to Egypt, God appears to Moses in 4:21–23 and lays out the mission. Pharaoh will be stubborn, but God will prevail. Pharaoh is strong-willed, but God is stronger. God can even shape Pharaoh's will. This is not predestination as we typically think of it. God did not foreordain Pharaoh's actions from eternity. Instead, God's words serve to bolster Moses' confidence as he prepares to confront a powerful and wicked king.

In Exodus 5, Moses and Aaron present Pharaoh with God's order, "Let my people go" (5:1). Pharaoh responds foolishly and defiantly: "Who is the LORD, that I should obey him and let Israel go? I do not know the LORD and I will not let Israel go" (5:2). His reply raises the stakes. Exodus becomes both a story of the liberation from injustice and illegitimate service and God's declaration to the earth of his identity, prestige, and power to save.

## The LORD Demonstrates His Power

God must encourage Moses and his people. Pharaoh doesn't just defy God; he intensifies the oppression of God's people by raising their daily work quota while simultaneously taking away their supplies. This act crushes the spirit of God's people and they turn on Moses (5:19–21). Moses complains to God, "Why, Lord, why have you brought this trouble on this people?" (5:22).

In Exodus 6:1–7:5, God reaffirms Moses' commission and mission. God's final words to Moses are telling:

> "But I will harden Pharaoh's heart, and though I multiply my signs and wonders in Egypt, he will not listen to you. Then I will lay my hand on Egypt and with mighty acts of judgment I will bring out my divisions, my people the Israelites. And the Egyptians will know that I am the LORD when I stretch out my hand against Egypt and bring the Israelites out of it." (7:3–5)

The goal of God's actions in Egypt is more than the liberation of God's people; it is *missional*. God wants the Egyptians to *know* him. This is remarkable. Pharaoh is a wicked and oppressive leader. Egypt has conspired with Pharaoh against God's people. Yet God still wants Egypt to *know* him. In fact, the LORD's grace is so limitless that he desires the whole earth to know him. This is a powerful reminder of why Israel exists. They are God's people through whom all peoples will be blessed (Gen. 12:3).

## Signs that Point to God

Pharaoh represents anti-creation and anti-humanity. Pharaoh is unbending in his evil actions. But God's mission must advance. The salvation of the world is at stake. God unleashes creation itself against Pharaoh and Egypt in order make himself *known* to Pharaoh, Egypt, Israel, and the world.

Exodus 7–10 details a series of nine signs, or plagues, that God sends against Egypt to gain the release of God's people. In rapid succession Moses and Aaron, through the power of God, turn water into blood, send swarms of frogs and insects, release plagues against Egypt's livestock, afflict the Egyptians with boils, unleash a devastating hailstorm, and cover the land with darkness. Profoundly, these signs demonstrate God's power and undermine the power of Pharaoh and gods of Egypt. Pharaoh was the personified sun god. His rule involved maintaining what the Egyptians called *Ma'at*. Ma'at was the balance, peace, justice, order, and tranquility present in the world. Pharaoh's role was to maintain this ideal state with the help of Egypt's gods. When God sends his signs, he is directly challenging the Ma'at of Egypt and Pharaoh's own prestige. Each sign challenges the power of Egypt's deities (Exod. 12:12). Thus, the LORD declares his true status at the expense of the false claims of Pharaoh and the gods. Who is the LORD? He is the true God of Egypt and of all creation. He alone is worthy of the title God.

The idea of God's identity recurs repeatedly throughout the showdown between the LORD and Pharaoh. God desires to be known. Pharaoh claims to be king, but in these texts it is God who demonstrates that the LORD is the true king and will reign forever and ever (Exod. 15:18).

## Hard Heart and Mission

We have a tendency to read about Pharaoh's hard heart and worry that this is how God works with all people. It isn't. Pharaoh was considered a deity. He was a god-king. He exercised his power for evil and not for good. Ultimately, God uses Pharaoh's own stubbornness as means of releasing his people and of revealing himself to the world. God humbles Pharaoh. Pharaoh is no god. He may not *know* the LORD, but the LORD knows him and uses Pharaoh's stubbornness as a means of *revealing* the true God to all the earth. Exodus 9:16 is clear: "But I have raised you up for this very purpose, that I might show you my power and that my name might be proclaimed in all the earth."

Thus, the exodus is a dramatic demonstration of God's power to save and advance his mission of extending blessing, goodness, and salvation to all peoples. Nothing can stop God's work in redeeming his broken creation and lost humanity—not even a powerful god-king. God rescued his people from illegitimate service to Pharaoh for exclusive service in God's kingdom.

## Questions for Reflection

What do you learn about God from his deliverance of Israel from Egypt?

_____

_____

From what do you need to be delivered?

_____

_____

From what does our world need to be delivered?

_____

_____

# DAY 4

# Passover and God's Victory

Exodus 12:21–42; 14:21–31; 15:1–18

*"Obey these instructions as a lasting ordinance for you and your descendants. When you enter the land that the LORD will give you as he promised, observe this ceremony. And when your children ask you, 'What does this ceremony mean to you?' then tell them, 'It is the Passover sacrifice to the LORD, who passed over the houses of the Israelites in Egypt and spared our homes when he struck down the Egyptians.'" Then the people bowed down and worshiped. The Israelites did just what the LORD commanded Moses and Aaron.—Exodus 12:24–28*

*Then Moses and the Israelites sang this song to the LORD: "I will sing to the LORD, for he is highly exalted. Both horse and driver he has hurled into the sea. The LORD is my strength and my defense; he has become my salvation. He is my God, and I will praise him, my father's God, and I will exalt him."—Exodus 15:1–2*

*"The LORD reigns for ever and ever."—Exodus 15:18*

---

**Core Truth:** Passover and the Red Sea crossing create holy memories to inspire and sustain the faith of God's people as they seek to live as his missional community.

---

The exodus from Egypt (12:1–15:21) is the grandest act of salvation in the Old Testament. It is memorialized in the Passover meal (12:1–13:16) and in an exuberant song of celebration for God's victory at the Red Sea (13:17–15:21, esp. 15:1–21).

## Passover

The Passover meal memorializes God's salvation of his people from Egypt. At the first Passover, God delivers his people and embeds it in their memory through a ceremonial meal. God instructs his people to prepare for deliverance by gathering as families to share in a sacred meal of roasted lamb and unleavened bread. They were to eat together wearing their travel clothes in anticipation of immediate departure from Egypt. Each part of the meal taught and reminded God's people of their experience as slaves. Each Israelite home ate lamb and put lamb blood on the doorframe. At midnight, God's angel passed through Egypt and killed the firstborn of every household not marked by the blood of a lamb.

Exodus 7–10 focuses on God's demonstration of power through nine signs to Pharaoh, Egypt, and God's people. Passover (see Exod. 11) is the final act that secures the release of God's people. The death of the firstborn is tragic but points to the costliness of deliverance and the devastation brought to human life through willful sin and stubborn disobedience. It is critical to remember that God acts for the sake of blessing all nations (including Egypt) through his people. In the New Testament, the climax of God's deliverance will be the sacrifice of Jesus, the Son of God, on the cross as the means of securing the salvation of the world.

After the original Passover, subsequent Passovers served as the annual celebration of the exodus. God's people used it to teach future generations. In the book of Exodus (12:1–13:16), the narrative of God's deliverance of his people is woven together with step-by-step instructions for future celebrations. *Memory* is critical for faith. *Remembering* God's past acts of grace grounds us in the present in anticipation of an abundant future.

## Victory at the Sea

At the Red Sea, God destroys the Egyptian army and guarantees the future of his people. Exodus includes both a narrative (13:17–14:31) and a poetic/ hymnic *celebration* of God's actions (15:1–21). As soon as Israel departs Egypt, Pharaoh changes his mind and sends out his chariots to overrun the Israelites. The Egyptians trap God's people on the shores of the Red Sea. But God saves Israel by unleashing the waters against the Egyptians.

God's use of the sea is a potent symbol. It is an act of creation. God brought forth dry land from the seas in his creative work in Genesis 1. The ancients feared water and saw it as a chaotic force that threatened the created world. The God of the exodus is so powerful, however, that he can deploy this elemental force as an instrument of deliverance. Simultaneously, God saves his people by creating a pathway through sea for them to cross to new life, and God is victorious against the forces of darkness that attempted to thwart his mission to extend blessing to all the nations. This victory guarantees the future and inspires his people to reverent faith (Exod. 14:30–31). God does for his people what they could not have done for themselves. God's people erupt in joyous celebration by singing of God's victory at the sea (15:1–21). This song worships God for *what God alone has done*. God acts in grace; God's people respond with worship grounded in *gratitude* for and *memory* of God's actions.

## Passover, Red Sea, and the Death and Resurrection of Jesus

Passover and the victory at the sea are critical for understanding Jesus' death and resurrection. These acts shaped God's Old Testament people, but they also foreshadowed Jesus' death and resurrection. It is no coincidence that Jesus' death will take place during the Passover of his day. Passover secured salvation for God's people; Jesus' death will secure the final means of salvation for all creation. During the Passover meal on the night of his betrayal, Jesus will inaugurate a new meal (the Lord's Supper/Eucharist/Communion) for his followers to share as a means of *remembering* and *grounding* themselves in his death.

But just as the initial deliverance from Egypt was incomplete without the final victory achieved at the Red Sea, so Jesus' sacrificial death takes on its fullest meaning in light of his resurrection on the third day. The Passover followed by God's victory at the Red Sea creates a key pattern that Jesus fulfills through his death on the cross and resurrection. Passover memorializes God's deliverance of his people from Egypt; the Lord's Supper memorializes his deliverance of the world from sin, injustice, and death through Jesus' sacrifice on the cross. The Red Sea announces God's victory over Egypt and guarantees the future of God's people; Jesus' resurrection declares God's ultimate victory over all the forces of sin, death, and injustice and guarantees the future for all who put their trust in Jesus. Jesus' followers live in light of Jesus' death and resurrection in anticipation of an abundant future guaranteed by God's victory through Jesus.

## Memory and Worship

Passover and the Red Sea establish patterns and habits for God's people. They ground our *spiritual* lives in the *historical* actions of God. They shape us by rooting us in the *memory* of God's gracious acts. The annual practice of Passover connects future generations to the exodus story. It also emphasizes *community* worship. God's people celebrate together. Worship is how God's people respond to grace. Worship focuses us on God. We live by the grace of God. He has done for us what we could never have done for ourselves. This recognition is crucial. Our lives point not to our own accomplishments but to the one who has saved us. This is our mission.

## Questions for Reflection

What are key events that have shaped your spiritual journey?

_____

_____

How do the Passover and Red Sea crossing function in the faith of God's people?

_____

_____

# DAY 5

# A Purposeful Deliverance

### Exodus 19:3–6

*Then Moses went up to God, and the LORD called to him from the mountain and said, "This is what you are to say to the descendants of Jacob and what you are to tell the people of Israel: 'You yourselves have seen what I did to Egypt, and how I carried you on eagles' wings and brought you to myself. Now if you obey me fully and keep my covenant, then out of all nations you will be my treasured possession. Although the whole earth is mine, you will be for me a kingdom of priests and a holy nation.' These are the words you are to speak to the Israelites."—Exodus 19:3-6*

> **Core Truth:** God delivers his people and encounters them at Sinai in order to commission them to live as his missional community to reflect his character in/to/for the world.

The exodus demonstrates God's power and willingness to save. The basis of God's salvation is in his grace and his desire to have a relationship. All of this also links to God's mission. God liberates his people from Egypt so that they are free to serve as a missional community for the sake of the world.

Exodus 19:3-6 summarizes the dynamic of Exodus. God's missional purposes for his people are made clear. Verses 3 and 6 frame God's invitation and calling by emphasizing that these are words for God's people. God has a multi-generational history with them. God defines the meaning and purpose of salvation by renewing their call to mission, holiness, and community.

## The Experience of Salvation

In verse four, God reminds Israel of his actions. The language is emphatic: "Your yourselves have seen." God addresses persons who have experienced his gracious power to save. Before we can talk mission, we have to talk about its roots in God's kindness and grace. We remember God's actions and then live in light of what he has done and will do. God grounds the future mission of his people in what he has done. What have his people seen?

God's people are recipients of abundant grace. First, God reminds them of the exodus. God ended Egypt's unjust rule and illegitimate oppression of them. God's powerful actions ended Egypt's oppression and sent a liberating message to the world: "that I may show you [Pharaoh] my power and that my name might be proclaimed in all the earth" (9:16). Slavery is now in the past. A new future opens for the people of God.

Second, God reminds, "how I carried you on eagles' wings" (19:4). God did for his people what they could not do for themselves. The imagery is majestic. God is like a mother eagle that protects and carries her eaglets. When young eagles are learning to fly, the mother eagle at times swoops under them and carries them through the air whenever their own strength fails.

Third, God guides his people to the holy mountain of Sinai: "and brought you to myself" (19:4). In our day, we assume that God loves and cares for people. In the ancient world, this was a radical idea. The Canaanite deity Baal had a holy mountain called Zaphon. Yet he did not invite people to his mountain—only other gods and goddesses came to visit him. Israel's God was unique. God welcomed his people to his mountain. This announcement would have gained the attention of the ancients. A god who is radically for us is profoundly good news.

God's actions in delivering Israel from Egypt and in carrying God's people to Sinai remind us that our life with God begins with grace. It is not what we have done to draw near to God; it is what God has done to bring us to himself.

## Response to Grace

How do we respond to grace? God has rescued his people and brought them to the sacred mountain Sinai/Horeb. God offers them relationship. This is the power of the "Now if" in verse 5. Israel has experienced God's grace. God invites Israel to respond *actively* by practicing faithful obedience within the context of covenant. We'll talk more specifically about covenant in the chapter 6. In short, covenant is a concept rooted in the ancient Near East. It was a formal treaty or agreement typically entered into by a great king with another nation.

At Sinai, the God who created the universe, made promises to Abraham and his descendants, and delivered his people from Egypt invites his people into covenant. Covenant is rooted in God's grace. But since relationships involve two parties, the recipient of grace must respond. Israel's response is to listen attentively to God and live faithfully.

## Special Status

If God's people accept his invitation to relationship, he will elevate them to a special status. Out of all the nations, God says that Israel will be his "treasured possession" or "precious heirloom" (v. 5). God has a mission for his people to fulfill. God's people must be secure in their standing with God. God's favoring of his own does not mean other nations are unimportant. In fact, verse 5 twice reminds us of the surrounding world: "out of all nations" and "the whole earth is mine." Living as treasured possession is a status for the sake of the rest of creation. It is not about lording over others; it is for the *service* of others. God wants us to be all in for his mission, so we must be confident of our standing with him.

## Commission to Mission

What does it mean to live as treasured possession? Verse 6 spells it out: God's people are a missional community that reflects and embodies God's character in/to/for the world. We discover GPS—(G)od's mission, (P)ersons in Community, and (S)pirit-transformed—again in the phrase "kingdom of priests and a holy nation." God's people are not a collection of soloists; they are a community. The words "kingdom" and "nation" remind us of the communal dimension of life. We are created for community. Israel is to embody this.

But they are not just any community. They are a community with a priestly function. What do priests do? They connect people to God. This is the function of God's people in the world. They are ambassadors of God's grace to others and teachers of God's truth. This is the role of a missional community. This text also reminds us of the necessity of holiness. God's people model his character through their life together.

## Questions for Reflection

How have you experienced God's grace in your life?

_____

_____

Do you know and feel that you are God's treasured possession?

_____

_____

Who is your mission?

_____

_____

Who is your community?

_____

_____

What does your life need to look like to live out this mission?

_____

_____

# Exodus, Liberation, and the Mission of God

## CORE TRUTHS

1. The LORD saved his oppressed people from Egypt for the sake of his mission to bless the nations.
2. The LORD calls, commissions, and equips Moses to serve as his agent of deliverance.
3. In the exodus from Egypt, God delivers his people and reveals his grace and power to save to the world.
4. Passover and the Red Sea crossing create holy memories to inspire and sustain the faith of God's people as they seek to live as his missional community.
5. God delivers his people and encounters them at Sinai in order to commission them to live as his missional community to reflect his character in/to/for the world.

## OPEN SESSION WITH PRAYER

## DEBRIEF THE READING FOR THE WEEK (15 MINUTES)

- What were the key takeaways that you gained from this week's reading?
- What aspects of the reading did you find confusing?
- What is the significance of the exodus and Red Sea crossing for Israel's faith?
- What is the purpose of God's deliverance of Israel from Egypt?

## WATCH VIDEO (30 MINUTES)

## CONVERSATION (15 MINUTES)

- What aspects of the message resonated with you most deeply?
- What questions did Brian's talk raise for you?
- The exodus served to secure Israel's present and future. What story currently serves to guide your life and provide you peace and security?
- What does the exodus teach us about our role in God's mission?
- From what does our world need to be delivered?

## CLOSING PRAYER

## CHAPTER SIX

# God's Holy Vision for His Missional People

At Sinai, the LORD reveals his vision for the life of God's people as his missional community for the world. Grounded in the deliverance from Egypt, the books of Exodus–Deuteronomy detail faithfulness as the key response of God's people to his grace. Faithfulness manifests itself in love for God and neighbor. These books also serve to warn God's people that unfaithfulness, especially idolatry and injustice, is the greatest threat to God's mission in the world.

# DAY 1

# Mission and God's Commandments

Read Exodus 20:1–17; Matthew 5:17–20, 43–48

*"I am the LORD your God, who brought you out of Egypt, out of the land of slavery. You shall have no other gods before me. You shall not make for yourself an image in the form of anything in heaven above or on the earth beneath or in the waters below. You shall not bow down to them or worship them; for I, the LORD your God, am a jealous God, punishing the children for the sin of the parents to the third and fourth generation of those who hate me, but showing love to a thousand generations of those who love me and keep my commandments. You shall not misuse the name of the LORD your God, for the LORD will not hold anyone guiltless who misuses his name."—Exodus 20:2-7*

---

**Core Truth:** As a response to his grace, God calls his people to reflect his character by faithfully loving God and neighbor.

---

Exodus 19:3–6 overviews God's vision for the life and mission of his people. In these verses, God invites his newly redeemed people into a covenant. Covenant is a core biblical concept. God had previously made covenants with Noah (Gen. 9) and Abraham (Gen. 17). It introduces the central covenant found in Genesis through Deuteronomy: the Sinai covenant. The Noahic covenant guaranteed the future of God's creation. The Abrahamic covenant promised perpetual descendants for Abraham. The Sinai covenant casts a vision of the holy missional community that God desires to advance his work in the world. Often, we misunderstand Israel's Scriptures as a set of rigid regulations.

Instead, we find at Sinai God's vision for life as a missional community that exists to reflect God's character in/to/for the nations.

## Covenant and Grace

Exodus 19:3–6 grounds the Sinai covenant in God's gracious deliverance from Egypt. Israel's standing is not based on its own strength or moral uprightness. God's people exist because of God's kindness, love, and grace. Faithfulness is Israel's response to grace. Israel does not earn God's love through its actions; it opens itself to more grace by responding in faithfulness to the God who saved them from Egyptian bondage.

In 19:5, God offers covenant, "If you obey me fully and keep my covenant." The Hebrew reads literally, "If you truly listen to my voice." Life with God involves receiving God's grace and responding to it positively through faithfully listening to his voice. This dynamic opens God's people up for more grace as he remakes us into the people whom he intends us to be. The specifics of Israel's response come in the following chapters. Faithfulness must be articulated for each subsequent generation so God offers a blueprint for creating a missional ethic in Exodus 20–23. In Exodus 20:1–17, God proclaims the Ten Commandments to his people from Mount Sinai/Horeb (cf. Deut. 5:6–21). These are ten broad statements of God's expectations for his people. Then, in Exodus 20:22–23:19, God offers more specific instructions that apply the Ten Commandments to concrete situations that they would face in their ancient Near Eastern context. Notice the movement from very general, to general, to more specific. As we seek to live faithfully, we must learn to listen to Scripture for our modern context as a means of reflecting God's character today.

## Five Principles for Hearing the Ten Commandments

1) The Ten Commandments begin by reminding us of God's grace. Exodus 20:2 is a reminder of what God has already done: "I am the LORD your God, who brought you out of Egypt, out of the land of slavery." Grace always precedes our response to God.

2) The Ten Commandments offer a holistic view of life. In the modern world, we compartmentalize by separating secular and spiritual. We assume

incorrectly a distinction between the spiritual and physical. The Ten Commandments hold these together. The Ten Commandments, as well as the rest of Scripture, summarize God's will as "Love God and Love Neighbor." Jesus affirms this when a Bible expert challenges him to declare the greatest commandment (Matt. 22:34–40). The implication of holding these together is profound. We do not truly love our neighbor if we do not love and honor God; we do not truly love God if we do not love and honor our neighbor. The truly spiritual life is intimately connected with how we live our lives moment by moment in relationship to God and others.

3) The opening commandments focus on idolatry as the greatest threat to our love for God. We love God by maintaining an exclusive and committed relationship with God. There can be no other gods in our lives. God allows for no divided loyalties. Of course this means that we must avoid confusing any part of creation with God or setting up any part of creation as a representation of God. Only humanity serves as God's image—nothing else (Gen. 1:26–31). One of the challenges of living in the twenty-first century is that the spirituality of the Western world has reduced God to the created world. For many, God is equivalent to the universe or Mother Earth. The God of Scripture is the Creator and thus cannot be reduced to any part of creation.

4) The second half of the Ten Commandments focuses on relationships with others: honoring parents, not killing others, not committing adultery, not stealing, not giving false witness, and not coveting another person or thing. It is important to remind ourselves that these are the *minimum* standards. In Matthew 5:17–48, Jesus teaches that the goal of these commands is not merely to establish a *minimum* but to point to a *maximum* of loving others as God does. Each of the Ten Commandments can be articulated in the positive. For example, take the command "You shall not steal" and reflect on what a community would look like that avoided stealing by practicing its opposite: *giving*. What does a community shaped by generosity look like? What kind of witness would it show to the world? When we begin to reflect on God's commandments in this way, we begin to model God's character to the watching world.

5) Sabbath provides the link between loving God and loving neighbor (Exod. 20:8–11). We honor God and keep Sabbath by refraining from work and simultaneously releasing others (including animals) from any obligations to work. Sabbath creates a holy space and models the integration of our love for God and our love for others and all creation.

## Questions for Reflection

What would your life look like if you lived out the ethic described in the Ten Commandments?

_____

_____

Rewrite the Ten Commandments (Exod 20:1–17) into specific positive statements (use "you shall" instead of "you shall not") using your own words to serve as a blueprint for your missional life.

_____

_____

# DAY 2

# Mission and the Promise of God with Us

### Exodus 40:34–38

*Then the cloud covered the tent of meeting, and the glory of the* Lord *filled the tabernacle. Moses could not enter the tent of meeting because the cloud had settled on it, and the glory of the* Lord *filled the tabernacle. In all the travels of the Israelites, whenever the cloud lifted from above the tabernacle, they would set out; but if the cloud did not lift, they did not set out—until the day it lifted. So the cloud of the* Lord *was over the tabernacle by day, and fire was in the cloud by night, in the sight of all the house of Israel during all their travels.—Exodus 40:34–38*

**Core Truth:** Salvation is freedom from bondage, but most profoundly it is freedom for relationship with God.

The God of Scripture desires to be in relationship with us. At creation, humanity was at the center of God's purposes. Disobedience and human brokenness marred God's original intentions, but with his calling of Abraham, he began advancing his mission to redeem humanity and heal creation through the calling of his people, Israel. Now that God has liberated Israel from Egyptian oppression and brought them into a covenant relationship at Sinai, he creates a means of dwelling in the midst of his people. God powerfully present with his people is the culmination of this new covenant.

The book of Exodus reaches its climax with the glory and awesomeness of God visibly filling the tabernacle (40:34–38). God's people are a "kingdom of priests" (19:6). Priests are mediators between God and humanity. When Israel was on the move, the tabernacle led the community into the world. When Israel camped, the tabernacle rested at the center of the community. This is a snapshot of missional community: God's people following him into the world and mediating his presence to the world through their lives.

## Tabernacle and Mission

First, it is important to note that the instructions for the building of the tabernacle (Exod. 25–31) and its construction (Exod. 35–40) dominate Exodus. There is more space devoted to the tabernacle than to any other narrative thread in Exodus. The tabernacle's completion and the arrival of God's indwelling presence serve as the climax to the book. Neither the crossing of the Red Sea nor the Ten Commandments is the climax of Exodus. Exodus is more about *freedom for* living as God's missional people than it is about *freedom from* Egyptian bondage. Just being free *from* something is not enough—we must live purposefully for God's glory and mission.

## Tabernacle as Gift

The tabernacle is a gift from God. The gods of Israel's neighbors had sacred mountains that were off-limits to people. Israel's God invited his people to his holy mountain (Sinai/Horeb). This demonstrates God's love for humanity and his desire for relationship. It expresses God's desire to be *with us*. Moreover, God actually creates a means by which his presence can accompany his people *everywhere*. God does not merely bring people to his mountain; he crafts a portable mountain that Israel can carry with them into the world on mission.

## Tabernacle and the Ministry of All

The tabernacle is the work of all God's people. God gives Moses instructions, and Moses follows them to the letter (Exod. 40:16). But it is the people of God who build the tabernacle. God inspires two master craftsmen, Bezalel and Oholiab, to guide the construction. They lead a crew of skilled workers. The remainder of God's people freely give material needed for the construction. God's people donate so much that Moses orders them to stop (36:5–6). The tabernacle requires huge amounts of gold, silver, bronze, and fine linen (38:21–31). The metals alone represent a vast fortune (more than one ton of gold, almost four tons of silver, and two and one-half tons of bronze). The support and gifts of God's people point ahead to the ministry of God's people in the New Testament (1 Cor. 12–14; Rom. 12).

## Tabernacle and the Spirit

The tabernacle foreshadows the work of the Holy Spirit in God's mission. It is the Spirit that empowers the work to its completion. The Spirit fills Bezalel (35:30–31) and provides an inspired assistant Oholiab (35:34). God also gave talents and gifts to many others in the community so that the skilled work could be done (36:1). Sometimes we think of the gifts of the Holy Spirit as only a New Testament phenomenon. The Spirit is much more prominent in the New Testament following Jesus' resurrection, but it is present here and works to advance God's mission.

## Tabernacle and God with Us

The tabernacle narrative reaches its climax in the experience of *God with us* as God's people move into the world on mission. God's glory comes to dwell with God's people, but his presence also rises up in the form of a cloud by day and fire by night in order to lead and guide the people toward the Promised Land. The invisible God whose real presence abides at the center of his people is reflected to the world through the lives of the community of faith.

The idea of "God with us" points forward to Jesus. Jesus will bring Israel's Scriptures to a climax and usher in the kingdom of God. If the tabernacle represented the *real* presence of God in the midst of his people, Jesus raises this reality to a higher level. John's gospel looks back on the tabernacle to make a profound statement about Jesus' coming. John 1:14 reads, "The Word became flesh and made his dwelling among us. We have seen his glory, the glory of the one and only Son, who came from the Father, full of grace and truth."

In the original Greek, the word translated "made his dwelling" is the verb form of the word for "tabernacle." Whereas God's glory was present but hidden within the innermost chamber of the tabernacle, God's glory manifested itself visibly in the incarnation. God took on the fullness of humanity in the person of Jesus to make the truth of God known to the world. Matthew's gospel reinforces this. Like John's gospel, *God with us* is linked to Jesus' coming as "Immanuel," i.e., "God with us" (Matt. 1:22–23). Matthew's gospel then concludes: "And surely I am with you always, to the very end of the age" (Matt. 28:20). This reminds us that God's real presence with his people is connected with God's mission of salvation. In Matthew, "God with us" is a reminder that the resurrected Jesus remains present to lead God's people into the world on mission.

## Questions for Reflection

What does God's desire for relationship with us teach us about his character?

_____

_____

What would it mean for you to live in a moment-by-moment relationship with the God of the Bible?

_____

_____

# DAY 3

# God's Grace and the Danger of Disobedience

### Read Exodus 32:1–14; 34:1–9

*When the people saw that Moses was so long in coming down from the mountain, they gathered around Aaron and said, "Come, make us gods who will go before us. As for this fellow Moses who brought us up out of Egypt, we don't know what has happened to him." Aaron answered them, "Take off the gold earrings that your wives, your sons and your daughters are wearing, and bring them to me." So all the people took off their earrings and brought them to Aaron. He took what they handed him and made it into an idol cast in the shape of a calf, fashioning it with a tool. Then they said, "These are your gods, Israel, who brought you up out of Egypt." When Aaron saw this, he built an altar in front of the calf and announced, "Tomorrow there will be a festival to the LORD." So the next day the people rose early and sacrificed burnt offerings and presented fellowship offerings. Afterward they sat down to eat and drink and got up to indulge in revelry.—Exodus 32:1–6*

*And he passed in front of Moses, proclaiming, "The LORD, the LORD, the compassionate and gracious God, slow to anger, abounding in love and faithfulness, maintaining love to thousands, and forgiving wickedness, rebellion and sin."—Exodus 34:6–7a*

---

**Core Truth:** Idolatry by God's people threatens their witness to the world and hampers God's mission through them.

The Bible does not whitewash life. Scripture recognizes the triumphs and tragedies of existence. God's mission is to bring salvation to a lost humanity and a broken world. The stakes are high. God has called people out of the chaos and catastrophe of Genesis 3–11 to serve as a missional community that reflects God's character in/to/for the world so that the nations may be blessed and the earth healed. In response, God's people must practice *faithful obedience*. When this does not happen, God's mission is compromised. Exodus 32–34 contains a grave warning about the dangers of disobedience. These chapters narrate a tragic tale of God's people turning from God to the futile worship of the image of the golden calf (32:1–6). While God speaks with Moses on Sinai, God's people build a golden idol in the shape of a calf and worship it as a replacement for the LORD. This rash act has immediate repercussions and threatens the existence of God's people. Profoundly, in the midst of tragic disobedience, it offers a reminder of the loving character of the God of the Scriptures.

## The Golden Calf in Israel's Story

Let's explore the context of the golden calf. It is sandwiched between the instructions for building the tabernacle (Exod. 25–31) and its actual construction (Exod. 35–40). This is intentional. The tabernacle account models the fruits of *faithfulness*. It describes all of Israel's work in constructing the tabernacle *exactly* as God had instructed Moses. The golden calf narrative (Exod. 32–34) reflects on the costs of *unfaithfulness* and *disobedience*. One way leads to life and the presence of God *with us*. The other brings death, purposelessness, and the absence of God. These contrasting paths call each generation of God's people to choose their road carefully. When Moses recasts God's vision for his people in the book of Deuteronomy, he calls the community to God's preferred position:

> "This day I call the heavens and the earth as witnesses against you that I have set before you life and death, blessings and curses. Now choose life, so that you and your children may live and that you may love the LORD your God, listen to his voice, and hold fast to him. For the LORD is your life, and he will give you many years in the land he swore to give to your fathers, Abraham, Isaac and Jacob." (Deut. 30:19–20)

God desires the absolute best for his people. This is the reason for including negative examples in Scripture. Scripture has lessons to teach as a means of shaping our lives in the *present*.

## Danger of Idolatry

Idolatry is the chief threat to Israel's continued existence. The Scriptures steadfastly resist any attempt to identify the LORD with an idol or image. Humanity created in the image of God is the only visible representation of God.

Moreover, this text reminds us of the ongoing danger of humanity's fall. Genesis 3–11 narrates the fall of humanity and describes the principal problem of human life today in the world. Exodus 32–34 tells the story of Israel's fall and serves as a prophetic witness against Israel's future acts of idolatry. God's mission requires the faithfulness of his people.

Sin threatens the very relationship between God and Israel, and it leads to punishment from Yahweh. There is grace (32:14), but they face consequences. Of course, God can forgive *any* sin, but sins, though forgivable, have consequences that can alter our lives. God will certainly forgive us. But every sin limits our freedom to live as the people whom God created us to be. The *graciousness of our God* who went to the cross for our sins is not a license to sin.

## Human Sin and God's Faithfulness

Despite the grave threat to God's mission posed by the golden calf, God relents and does not destroy Israel (32:14) and he restarts the mission with Moses alone (32:10). God's promises to Abraham, Isaac, and Israel play a role in this. Throughout Genesis and Exodus, God faithfully fulfills his promises despite the actions of humanity. This is good news. Salvation is the work of God and not the work of God's people. Human sin is serious business but it will not thwart God's desire to redeem the world through the life, death, and resurrection of Jesus.

## Spiritual Leadership and Prayer

Despite the failings of Israel, Moses vigorously advocates on their behalf to God. Exodus 32:11–13 is actually the first of four scenes of intercessory prayer by Moses within the chapters of Exodus 32–34 (32:11–13; 32:31–32; 33:12–18; and 34:8–9). In 32:11–13, Moses serves as a mediator and pleads with God to be merciful and forgive his wayward people. In these chapters, Moses continues to intercede until God assures Moses that he will indeed both forgive and accompany Israel to the Promised Land. Moses models for us a crucial role for spiritual leadership in our day. If we find ourselves leading others in a spiritual community, it is vital that we pray regularly for our community as well as the wider world.

## Love as God's Core Characteristic

Exodus 32–34 is foundational for the Old Testament's portrait of God. In the aftermath of the sin of the golden calf, Israel experiences the fullness of God's character—God at his core is gracious and merciful. God forgives Israel because this is central to who God is: "The LORD, the LORD, the compassionate and gracious God, slow to anger, abounding in love and faithfulness, maintaining love to thousands, and forgiving wickedness, rebellion and sin" (34:6–7a). Moses is successful in his prayers and God relents because it is his nature to forgive!

## Questions for Reflection

What are the greatest challenges to faithfulness in your life?

_____

_____

How would your life change if you knew God truly loved you and desires to forgive you?

_____

_____

Do you believe that God stands ready and willing to forgive you right now?

_____

_____

# Loving God:
# The Great Commandment

Read Deuteronomy 6:4–25; Matthew 22:35–40

*Hear, O Israel: The L*ORD *our God, the L*ORD *is one. Love the*
L*ORD *your God with all your heart and with all your soul*
*and with all your strength.—Deuteronomy 6:4–5*

*Jesus replied: "'Love the Lord your God with all your heart and with all your*
*soul and with all your mind.' This is the first and greatest commandment.*
*And the second is like it: 'Love your neighbor as yourself.' All the Law and*
*the Prophets hang on these two commandments."—Matthew 22:37–40*

> **Core Truth:** God desires the total devotion and love of his people as
> our response to his kindness and graciousness.

God's vision is for his people to serve as a missional community that reflects and embodies his character in/to/for the world. We respond to God's grace with faithfulness rooted in devotion to him. This is the message of the Shema, or Great Commandment, in Deuteronomy 6:4–5 (cf. Matt. 22:35–40; Mark 12:28–31; Luke 10:25–28). It calls God's people to realign themselves continually in terms of their allegiance to the God who delivered them.

## The LORD Is Our God

Deuteronomy 6:4 opens with a call: "Hear" or "Pay attention." The declaration, "The LORD our God," follows. Remember that "LORD" is not a title but a reverent way of saying God's name, "Yahweh." Yahweh is the name revealed to Moses on Sinai. Recall also that Israel lived in a context of many gods with competing stories. The spirituality of God's people rests on their communal commitment to the true God. This is not a personalized spirituality or faith separated from a community. Our text reads, "Yahweh is *our* God," rather than, "Yahweh is *my/his/hers/their* god." Individual faith must manifest itself within a community. God's people are a missional *community*. The ethic of the Bible is a spirituality and life that connects the relationship with the Divine to our relationship with creation and especially with other people.

## The LORD Is One

The Shema declares the full implications of "The LORD is our God" in the next phrase: "The LORD is one" or "The LORD alone." Declaring that the LORD is one means that we affirm that the LORD and he alone is our God. God does not allow for divided loyalties. Such an affirmation was critically important in Israel's polytheistic environment. It remains vital today. North America is as pluralistic and polytheistic as the ancient Near East. Religions with vastly different understandings of the Divine are present in increasing numbers, especially in large urban areas. The popular spirituality of North America is a mixture of various faiths. In our culture, you will hear the words *God, Jesus, Mother Earth, the universe, Allah*, or *goddess* used interchangeably for the Divine. Spirituality becomes a supermarket cereal aisle—many colorful and diverse choices, but at the core made of the same stuff. The biblical understanding of God is radically different. In its polytheistic context, the Bible argues for the incomparability of the LORD to any other competing claim about the gods (cf. Exod. 15:11). The LORD alone is worthy of the title "God" because the LORD stands alone and above all other religious and spiritual claims.

The polytheism of the modern world also comes in the form of ideologies, addictions, and desires. Sex, money, and power are gods for many. Allegiance to political ideologies often reaches the fervor of religious commitment—ironically often at the expense of clear biblical teaching. The Shema testifies to the faith community of its ultimate allegiance. We must remain sensitive to the subtle allure of competing gods and make God our Lord over all aspects of life: spiritual, ethical, relational, financial, political, and sexual.

## Total Devotion

What does God ask of those seeking to align with his ways? It is more than a declaration of faith or clinging to a set of rules. God calls for us to respond with *total devotion*. God calls for us to love him. God wants an authentic relationship with every man and woman. Loving God is our response to his grace. In 6:4, we noted the *communal* dimension. The LORD is *our* God. In 6:5, the emphasis becomes the *individual* response of each person within the community. God calls each of us to love God with all of *his* or *her* heart, soul, and strength. Our corporate witness as God's people resounds through the chorus of each individual voice.

What does it mean to love God? To love God is more than affection or warm feelings. It is a *devoted commitment* that involves our whole being. The Shema uses a three-fold response. God calls us to love him with all our heart, soul, and strength. The intent is not to divide a person into three spheres as though the Great Commandment is referring to a person's emotional life (heart), spiritual life (soul), and physical life (strength). This is a misunderstanding rooted in an incorrect reading of these words. In Hebrew, *heart* points to our inner world of thought, will, and intention. It does not carry the emotional connotations of heart as our English expression, "I love you with all of my heart" conveys. The New Testament's use of *mind* captures the intent of the Hebrew well. Likewise, *soul* does not refer to a spiritual part of a person that can be separated from the physical body. In Hebrew, *soul* refers to the totality and essence of a person.

Our response to God involves a devoted commitment to God involving *all* of our thoughts/will/intentions and *all* that we are as persons. Simply loving God with all of our thoughts and intentions would be significant. Adding *soul* brings us to a 100 percent commitment. Instead of thinking of these terms as parts of person, consider them overlapping circles with *heart* in the center and *soul* encompassing *heart,* but adding all of the rest of a person. This is *total* devotion. The Shema is a call for a whole-person response of commitment to God with all of our thoughts, intentions, talents, and giftedness. Yet the Shema adds a third element: *strength.* In Hebrew, the phrase reads "and all your very much." If we are already at 100 percent devotion, what is left to give? I think that the Shema adds this to intensify our calling. The expression "Give 110 percent" captures some of the meaning here.

God saves his people. The Shema reminds us that our response is living all in for God.

## Questions for Reflection

What would it take to raise your commitment to God to 110 percent?

_____

_____


What other gods do you need to lay aside today to fully commit to the God who created you and loves you?

_____

_____

# DAY 5

# Loving Neighbor: Practicing Justice for All

Read Exodus 20:22–21:11; book of Philemon

*"But love your neighbor as yourself. I am the LORD."—Leviticus 19:18b*

---

**Core Truth:** God's people live out their love of God by lovingly practicing justice for people, animals, and the environment.

---

To love one's neighbor is the second core command in the Scripture. It appears for the first time in Leviticus 19:18b: "but love your neighbor as yourself. I am the LORD." If our spiritual life finds its roots in an exclusive relationship with our God, then it finds its clearest moment-by-moment expression through how we treat other people, animals, and the environment. Justice is central to Scripture. The entrance of sin (Gen. 3–11) morphed God's creation from a place of peace and wholeness (Gen. 1–2) to an arena of brokenness and injustice. In God's future, there will be relational wholeness in humanity on three levels: God and humanity, men with women, and humanity and creation. God's mission involves working to restore the God–human relationship with a goal of healing all creation.

## Equal Justice for All Creation

In Israel's legal materials (Exod. 20–23; Lev. 18–23; and Deut. 12–26), the treatment of others is central to how God's people manifest his character. In particular, protections for the poor and marginalized in society dominate the discourse. In our modern world, it is easy to be cynical about the ability of the wealthy and/or well-connected to dominate. Human history offers a repeating narrative of oppression of the majority by elites. Ancient law codes such as Hammurabi's Code (Hammurabi was king in Babylon 1792–1750 BCE, a few centuries before the exodus) mandated different punishments and outcomes depending on a person's social status. The later Roman Empire would have a similar multi-tiered justice system. God's vision for humanity is different. For God's people, there is no favoritism. Rich and poor alike enjoy equal protection under God's law. This is rooted in core Old Testament ideals.

Israel's view of justice finds its roots in creation. As we've seen, God created all people (men and women alike) in his image. All means all. It is not merely the wealthy, politically powerful, and the well-connected who bear God's image, but the stranger, the widow, and the orphan. The Sabbath commandment (Exod. 20:8–11) exemplifies this by linking Sabbath rest for all with creation.

Israel's view of justice gains traction by continual reminders of life in Egypt. Life in Egypt is now the past once God delivers his people through the exodus, but liberating God's people from Egypt was easier than getting Egypt out of Israel. In core reminders such as Exodus 20:2, God self-identifies as "I am the LORD your God, who brought you out of Egypt, out of the land of slavery" (cf. Deut. 5:6). Egypt functions as a negative example for the loving and just relationships that God's people are to model: "And you are to love those who are foreigners, for you yourselves were foreigners in Egypt" (Lev. 19:34; cf. Deut. 10:19). Scripture is emphatic that God's people are not to mimic the status quo of the nations. God's people are to reflect the values and ethos of God's kingdom.

## Loving Neighbor by Protecting the Marginalized

The detailed law code called "The Book of the Covenant" (Exod. 20:22–23:33) opens with laws concerning the worship of God (20:22–26) and the practice of slavery (21:1–11). These two topics reaffirm the love God/love neighbor ethos that God seeks to instill in his people. By dealing upfront with the cultural practice of slavery, the Book of the Covenant announces that its vision for God's people includes substantial protections for those most at risk for marginalization and abuse. These laws shape a vision for a community that practices justice, mercy, and wholeness. The presence of laws about slavery offends many modern readers. But these laws remind God's people that his vision of justice impacts every aspect of life. God is God of all. God's mission is to redeem creation. Thus, God engages human culture in all of its messiness. This begins with God's people. Rather than lamenting the presence of slavery in the Scriptures, we may want to reflect what it would mean if Scripture did not address a commonly practiced institution that continues in force into our day. By the time we get to the New Testament, the entire book of Philemon was written to encourage a slave-owning Christian to receive a runaway slave back as a *brother*. This is a vision of a world without slavery.

## Sinai's Vision for God's People: Loving Our Neighbor

Let's reflect on the power of practicing love of neighbor, especially the marginalized.

First, Israel's legal materials offer protection to aliens, widows, orphans, and slaves. Unlike the surrounding nations, whose laws privileged the ruling classes, the Sinai laws did not have different punishments based on the class of the guilty person. Moreover the Sinai materials specifically name marginalized groups and thus consciously create a counter-narrative to the human experience of oppression and advantage. God's people are to take care of those who are in need.

Second, the experience of God's people in Egypt serves as the basis for an ethos of non-oppression. Nelson Mandela, former president of South Africa, wrote, "For to be free is not merely to cast off one's chains, but to live in a way that respects and enhances the freedom of others."[8] These words reflect the vision of God's mission. Israel, as God's people, have a story rooted in grace, but its power as a witness to the nation turns on the degree to which God's people practice love for neighbor.

Last, God cares for the marginalized. God hears their cries and has deep compassion (Exod. 2:24; 22:23, 27). Thus, rooted in God's vision for life is the expectation that God's people will practice justice. This vision does not permit us to separate our spirituality from how we treat others. God's laws remind us that our spiritual life is intimately related to the manner in which we live moment by moment.

Jesus will model these principles in his life. Religions tend to comfort the comfortable. The Bible provides true comfort and compassion for all, including the oppressed. This is good news.

## Questions for Reflection

How do you practice justice in your daily life?

_____

_____

Who is your neighbor?

_____

_____

How is God calling you to act for the poor and marginalized in your city or neighborhood?

_____

_____

# God's Holy Vision
# for His Missional People

## CORE TRUTHS

1. As a response to his grace, God calls his people to reflect his character by faithfully loving God and neighbor.
2. Salvation is freedom from bondage, but most profoundly it is freedom for relationship with God.
3. Idolatry by God's people threatens their witness to the world and hampers God's mission through them.
4. God desires the total devotion and love of his people as our response to his kindness and graciousness.
5. God's people live out their love of God by lovingly practicing justice for people, animals, and the environment.

## OPEN SESSION WITH PRAYER

## DEBRIEF THE READING FOR THE WEEK (15 MINUTES)

- What were the key takeaways that you gained from this week's reading?
- What aspects of the reading did you find confusing?
- Summarize God's desired response from his people to his grace.
- What does God's desire for relationship with us teach us about his character?
- How does the golden calf threaten God's mission?

## **WATCH VIDEO** (30 MINUTES)

## **CONVERSATION** (15 MINUTES)

- What aspects of the message resonated with you most deeply?
- What questions did Brian's talk raise for you?
- How does God desire our community to live?
- What type of witness does community shaped by the Ten Commandments offer to the world?
- What are the greatest challenges to faithfulness that we face in our world?
- What does it mean to love God?
- How is God calling us to act for the poor and marginalized in our cities or neighborhoods?

## **CLOSING PRAYER**

## CHAPTER SEVEN

# Israel's Life in the Land: The Potential and Pitfalls of Living as God's Missional People

Following the vision for God's people in Genesis–Deuteronomy, the books of Joshua–Nehemiah tell the story of Israel's life in the land. The descendants of Abraham and Sarah were to live as God's missional people for the sake of the nations. Israel's story documents the potential and pitfalls of living as God's missional people. These books serve as a warning against unfaithfulness in the form of idolatry and injustice. These books also introduce us to the role that God's king, or Messiah, will play in God's mission and remind us of God's desire for relationship with humanity through the building of his temple in Jerusalem. Unfaithfulness ultimately leads to exile from the land, but God remains faithful to his people and mission. Israel's story will end in a return from exile and the anticipation of God's future work of salvation through the life, death, and resurrection of Israel's Messiah, Jesus.

# DAY 1

# Israel's Golden Generation

### Read Joshua 24:1–28

*After the death of Moses the servant of the LORD, the LORD said to Joshua son of Nun, Moses' aide: "Moses my servant is dead. Now then, you and all these people, get ready to cross the Jordan River into the land I am about to give to them—to the Israelites. I will give you every place where you set your foot, as I promised Moses. Your territory will extend from the desert to Lebanon, and from the great river, the Euphrates—all the Hittite country—to the Mediterranean Sea in the west. No one will be able to stand against you all the days of your life. As I was with Moses, so I will be with you; I will never leave you nor forsake you. Be strong and courageous, because you will lead these people to inherit the land I swore to their ancestors to give them. Be strong and very courageous. Be careful to obey all the law my servant Moses gave you; do not turn from it to the right or to the left, that you may be successful wherever you go. Keep this Book of the Law always on your lips; meditate on it day and night, so that you may be careful to do everything written in it. Then you will be prosperous and successful. Have I not commanded you? Be strong and courageous. Do not be afraid; do not be discouraged, for the LORD your God will be with you wherever you go."—Joshua 1:1–9*

---

**Core Truth:** The courage to listen to Scripture and practice faithfulness are the keys that unlock the future for God's people.

---

Joshua 1:1–9 sets the tone for the entire book of Joshua. The LORD speaks directly to Joshua, Moses' successor. This text is critical for understanding the call and vocation of God's people as we seek to live as his missional community that reflects God's character in/to/for the world.

## Dynamic Future

God's mission involves establishing his people in the land of Canaan in fulfillment of his promises to Abraham, Isaac, and Jacob. Following the exodus, it is now time for God's people to return to the Promised Land and live there. God grants Joshua an expanded vision of this life. He will guide God's people to inhabit every place where his feet touch. God promises his presence and guarantees success.

## Courageous Faithfulness

But God's graciousness requires a response. Joshua must actually walk into the Promised Land. Joshua must lead Israel well. He must be strong and courageous.

In Hebrew, *strong* and *courageous* are two closely related terms. Joshua needs to be a person of strong resolve. Strength and courage in this context point to a resolve to accomplish God's will. Without the courage to act on God's will, Joshua's calling cannot be fulfilled.

"Be strong and courageous" repeats three times in verses 6–9. The first and the last repetitions explain why courage is necessary. The middle repetition (vv. 7–8) describes how one may cultivate and embody courage. Verse 6 provides the first reason. Joshua is God's chosen leader *for the people in fulfillment of God's plan.* Joshua has been called to live for something profoundly greater than his own self-interest. He has been called to *lead* God's people into the Promised Land—a land that God had promised generations ago to Abraham, Isaac, and Jacob. Joshua's generation will be the one to enjoy the fulfillment of this promise *but* Joshua must be strong and courageous.

Verse 9 offers the second reason. God will be *with* Joshua. God's presence with Joshua and his people removes any reason for fear. The language here is a warning against being paralyzed or demoralized by fear. This doesn't mean that Joshua (or we) will never *feel* afraid. Instead, these words exhort Joshua to act courageously because of God's presence. This is important. Courage is not the absence of fear. Fear is normal. A godly courage unleashes an individual to act on behalf of others in spite of fear. This connects courage directly with holiness, which involves moving from a life centered on self to a life focused on service to others. This was Joshua's call.

## Rooted in the Word

It is illuminating to ponder Joshua's part in advancing God's mission. God is calling him to a courageous faithfulness in verses 7–8. Notice the extra emphasis here: "Be strong and *very* courageous." The two middle verses describe the key to courage—being shaped moment by moment by Scripture. Joshua does not receive any special training as a political or military leader. The key to his fulfilling God's mission is a life of *faithful obedience*. He is to live and lead God's people faithfully. If he follows the way of Scripture, he and all of Israel will experience prosperity and success. For Joshua, courage involves more than personal valor; it involves the resolve and commitment to read the Word and live it out. Meditating and living God's Word was to serve as the moment-by-moment vocation for Joshua (Josh. 1:8; cf. Ps. 1:2). This is the way of life for God's people. In Deuteronomy 17:14–20, God describes the ideal king for his people through Moses. At its heart lies a call for the king to be a man shaped and formed by God's Word.

## Success

God guarantees Joshua and his people success as long as they practice faithfulness. The rest of the book of Joshua narrates Israel's triumphant return to the land first promised to Abraham, Isaac, and Jacob. God fulfills his promises and his people are able to settle in the Promised Land—Canaan. Joshua 21:43–45 summarizes the success of God's people. Joshua 21:45 testifies to God's faithfulness: "Not one of all the LORD's good promises to Israel failed; every one was fulfilled."

## Israel's Mission

It may seem odd to talk about God's mission in a book full of battle stories in which God's people are fighting against other nations in the land of Canaan. But Joshua is about setting the scene for the advance of God's mission through the establishment of his kingdom. Israel does not exist against the nations. As we've seen, God has called Israel to serve as a new humanity for the sake of the nations. This includes even the nations that may rise up and openly oppose God's mission such as Pharaoh's Egypt or the Canaanite nations in the book of Joshua. God desires to save all of humanity so he must protect his people as the human agents through whom he will extend blessing to the rest of humanity (Gen. 12:3; cf. Exod. 19:5–6). Even in Joshua there is hope for the nations. Rahab and her family align with the LORD (Josh. 2:8–14; 6:22–25) and are saved from Jericho's destruction. The Gibeonites also make peace with God's people and live side by side with Israel (see Josh. 9).

## Call to Faithfulness

Israel's position as the privileged people of God is rooted in grace, but the relationship must be nurtured and grown through faithfulness. Joshua and his generation model a courageous faithfulness. This generation is the model for all subsequent generations of God's people. God's mission depends in part to our response to grace. Joshua's generation was great because it listened to God's voice and lived out the mission. How will we live?

## Questions for Reflection

Do you think that your future can be as abundant and dynamic as Joshua's?

_____

_____

Do you have the courage to read the Scriptures and live them out?

_____

_____

What fears keep you from following God?

_____

_____

What would a community look like that continually realigned itself with Scripture?

_____

_____

# DAY 2

# Tragedy in the Promised Land

Read Judges 2:6–3:6; 21:25

*After Joshua had dismissed the Israelites, they went to take possession of the land, each to their own inheritance. The people served the LORD throughout the lifetime of Joshua and of the elders who outlived him and who had seen all the great things the LORD had done for Israel. Joshua son of Nun, the servant of the LORD, died at the age of a hundred and ten. And they buried him in the land of his inheritance, at Timnath Heres in the hill country of Ephraim, north of Mount Gaash. After that whole generation had been gathered to their ancestors, another generation grew up who knew neither the LORD nor what he had done for Israel. Then the Israelites did evil in the eyes of the LORD and served the Baals. They forsook the LORD, the God of their ancestors, who had brought them out of Egypt. They followed and worshiped various gods of the peoples around them. They aroused the LORD's anger.—Judges 2:6–12*

*In those days Israel had no king; everyone did as they saw fit.—Judges 21:25*

---

**Core Truth:** Each generation must renew and nurture its relationship with God in order to serve faithfully as God's missional people.

---

The book of Joshua marked Israel at its best. Under Joshua, God's people practiced faithfulness and they experienced success in advancing God's mission in the world. The generation of Joshua serves as a witness to faithfulness.

Astonishingly, the generations following Joshua's will serve as a warning against disobedience. The book of Judges tells the story of what happens when God's people forsake their allegiance to the LORD. God's mission does not merely come to a standstill. It actually reverses course and takes several steps backward. How was it possible for God's people to turn away from the successes and blessings of faithful obedience so quickly?

## The Allure of Idols

God's people return to a familiar pattern. At the heart of God's covenant with his people is God's desire for authentic relationship. The ethos that God desires for humanity is clear: love God and love others. The life of God's dreams begins and ends with a whole-being commitment to God. Yet as the Bible witnesses, it is the ongoing challenge of human existence to practice faithfulness.

Judges 2:6–9 reminds the reader of the triumphs and faithfulness of Joshua and his generation. Yet 2:10 ominously announces a new reality: "After that whole generation had been gathered to their ancestors, another generation grew up who knew neither the LORD nor what he had done for Israel." God desires for his people (and all nations) to know him, but the Scriptures warn that this knowledge must be embraced and renewed continually. Each generation of God's people must realign itself. It cannot rest on the successes of previous generations or assume that they gain merit from their parents.

Lacking a knowledge of the true God is not a neutral position. Humans will always fill the need for the Divine with something. If it is not the Creator, it will inevitably be some part of creation. Judges tells the story of God's people turning to the worship and allegiance of the gods of the nations.

## The Cycle of Disobedience

The result of not knowing God and turning to idols is a downward cycle of spiritual defeat. The book of Judges describes a cycle of disobedience that replays throughout the time of the Judges. It begins with Israel failing to know God and/or forgetting God. This failure leads them to pursue other gods and goddesses. In response, God removes his protection from his people and allows other nations to harass and oppress them. God then sends a deliverer in the form of a powerful warrior/leader called a judge. Once the judge saves God's people and restores order and abundance, God returns his favor to Israel. This cycle continues throughout the book of Judges. Judges 2:6–3:6 describes this pattern. Judges 3:7–16:31 tells the stories of the men and women who served as judges during this troubled era for God's people.

## Legendary Judges of Israel

The judges whom God raises up to deliver his people are some of the most memorable characters in the Bible. Their names include Gideon, Samson, and Deborah. These judges lead God's people to great victories, but there is also a darker side to some of them. The initial judges Othniel, Ehud, and Deborah (3:7–5:31) deliver Israel and model commitment to God's mission throughout their life. The last series of major judges—Gideon, Jephthah, and Samson (6:1–16:31)—are a mixed bag of good and bad. They all deliver God's people from enemies but spiritual and moral chaos engulf their lives. After winning a great victory, Gideon makes an ephod (a false religious symbol), and God's people end up worshiping it rather than the LORD (8:27). Jephthah delivers Israel and then sacrifices his own daughter as a means of fulfilling a vow (11:39). The entire narrative of Samson is tragic because he repeatedly makes poor moral decisions while at the same time fighting against Israel's enemies (13:1–16:31). The judges suggest that leadership is important but that it is also dependent on the character and commitment of the individual leader.

## Chaos in Need of a King

The book of Judges ends with a series of troubling narratives that capture the depths to which God's people have fallen (Judges 17–21). These are disturbing stories of idolatry, violence, rape, and civil war among the tribes of God's people. Framing these narratives of chaos, horror, and violence is a recurring refrain: "In those days Israel had no king" (18:1; 19:1; 21:25). The final recurrence adds an additional word of explanation: "In those days Israel had no king; everyone did as they saw fit" (21:25). Chaos reigned due to a lack of godly leadership and direction. The world of Genesis 3–11 returns in force. God's people act out of their own strength and tragically follow their impulses rather than continuing to practice the faithfulness modeled by Joshua.

The solution to unfaithfulness according to the book of Judges is a faithful leader who will guide God's people to a courageous faithfulness. It will be a person who follows, digests, and embodies God's Word. Joshua served in this role for an earlier generation. In the books of First and Second Samuel and First and Second Kings, we will discover the role and potential of the king. The key question for God's people will be this: What kind of king is needed? The

Scriptures will paint a profound picture of what kingship looks like for God's people. It will be Jesus alone who fills this role to the fullest potential of what God intended.

## Questions for Reflection

Compare and contrast the generation of Joshua with the generations described in the book of Judges.

_____

_____

What warnings does the book of Judges provide for us today who wish to live for God?

_____

_____

Why do you think the Israelites turned so quickly from the model of Joshua's generation?

_____

_____

# DAY 3

# Longing for a Messiah

Read Deuteronomy 17:14–20; 2 Samuel 7:5–16; Psalm 2

*"I will also give you rest from all your enemies. The LORD declares to you that the LORD himself will establish a house for you: When your days are over and you rest with your ancestors, I will raise up your offspring to succeed you, your own flesh and blood, and I will establish his kingdom. He is the one who will build a house for my Name, and I will establish the throne of his kingdom forever. I will be his father, and he will be my son. When he does wrong, I will punish him with a rod wielded by men, with floggings inflicted by human hands. But my love will never be taken away from him, as I took it away from Saul, whom I removed from before you. Your house and your kingdom will endure forever before me; your throne will be established forever."—2 Samuel 7:11–16*

> **Core Truth:** God's ideal ruler or Messiah will lead God's people to fulfill his mission by living out faithfully the message of Scripture.

After the period of the judges, Israel moves into the era of monarchy. From roughly 1040 BC until 587 BC, kings ruled over God's people. Will kingship inspire and lead God's people to fully live out their vocation as a missional community that reflects God's character in/to/for the nations? Can they embrace faithfulness (love for God and neighbor) over idolatry and injustice?

## The Biblical Model for Kingship

In the ancient Near East, kingship appeared around 3000 BC. Both the Sumerians (located in the southern part of modern Iraq) and the Egyptians had kings. A powerful central ruler whose reign was blessed by the gods became a common feature of the ancient world. Kings had the ability to draft workers for forced-labor projects, keep large harems of women for their own pleasure, amass fortunes through taxation and control over commerce, and maintain authority through military power. They created and protected a status quo that favored themselves and other elites in society. The king was the law.

God permits his people to have a king (Deut. 17:14–20), but Israel's king stands in contrast to the kings of the nations in key ways. Unlike the kings of the nations, Israel's king was not to amass wealth, women, or weapons of war (Deut. 17:16–17).

Most fundamentally, the LORD was the true King of God's people (Exod. 15:18; 1 Sam. 12:12; Isa. 6:5). God as King established his law at Sinai by which God's people, including the king, lived. In other words, the Israelite king ruled under the authoritative guidance of Scripture. He did not create the law; he administered the law on behalf of God. The king's primary role was to copy God's law (Scripture) and study it continually. He was to lead God's people by faithfully listening to and living out the Scriptures. As we saw, Joshua led God's people in this fashion (Josh. 1:1–9). The king was God's human agent through whom God administered his kingdom.

## David, the Man after God's Own Heart

Israel's first king was Saul. He ruled from roughly 1040–1000 BC. He failed to follow God obediently (2 Sam. 13–15) so God chose a new king—David. David, along with Moses, is one of the central figures in the Old Testament. His significance carries into the New Testament; Jesus will be called "Son of David" (Matt. 1:1).

First Samuel 13–2 Kings 2 records the life, reign, and death of David. The core value that separated David from Saul and set him up as the model king was his heart for God (1 Sam. 13:14). As we saw in Deuteronomy 6:4–5, *heart* refers to the center of a person's thinking and will. David was all in for God. This does not mean that David was perfect; he was not, but David was committed to God's mission and sought to center and order his life around God's plans and purposes. David unified Israel following Saul's death, gained victory over the enemies of God's people, and brought the Ark of the Covenant to reside permanently in Jerusalem (2 Sam. 1–6). David's heart for God became the model for all future kings over God's people.

## The Davidic Covenant

Second Samuel 7:11–16 is a critically important passage of the Old Testament. In these verses, God makes a generous promise to David and his descendants in the form of a covenant. God promises David a perpetual descendent who would serve as his human agent to advance his kingdom. The Davidic covenant is the last of major covenants in the Old Testament. It establishes David as the paradigm for the king in God's kingdom. Just as God promised Abraham perpetual descendants, the Davidic covenant guarantees that David's descendants will always reign.

## The Failure of Israel's Kings

Tragically, Israel's human kings failed to live up to their calling and mission. Of all of Israel's kings, only a few received the approval of the biblical writers: David, Asa, Hezekiah, and Josiah. All of the others, including Solomon who will build the temple, failed as kings because of their lack of faithfulness in serving God wholeheartedly. After Solomon's reign, the unified Israel split in two: a northern kingdom (Israel) and a southern kingdom (Judah). The books of 1 and 2 Kings trace the fall of both of these kingdoms.

First and 2 Kings judge all of the northern kings as evil rulers because they did not keep God's people in the north from the idolatry caused by the first northern king: Jeroboam son of Nebat (1 Kings 12–14). Jeroboam had set up two golden calves for worship in the cities of Dan and Bethel (1 Kings 12:25–33). All of his successors permitted this apostasy to continue. The result of this unfaithfulness was the northern kingdom's destruction by the Assyrian Empire in 722 BC.

Sons of David ruled over Judah. Sadly, the southern kingdom enjoyed only a few "good" kings. Of these, only Josiah explicitly administered the kingdom by listening to Scripture. Faithfulness to the book of the law is only mentioned during his reign (2 Kings 22–23). Josiah led a vigorous reform of God's people, but his successors quickly undid his good and Judah fell to the hands of the Babylonians in 587 BC, ending the reign of the house of David.

## The Hope of Messiah

The promises to David served as the source of hope for God's people even after the disaster of 587 BC. God's people continued to pray to God to restore his kingdom through a new king or Messiah. The book of Psalms is full of songs about the Davidic king (e.g., Psalms 2 and 110). When God's people prayed these, they anticipated the day when a new Messiah would emerge and liberate God's people once again. It is this hope that Jesus the Messiah (Christ) fulfilled when he announced the kingdom of God at the beginning of his ministry.

## Questions for Reflection

How well do you listen to the Scriptures and live out the values of the kingdom of God?

_____

_____

What would need to change for you to be known as a man or woman after God's own heart?

_____

_____

How does understanding kingship in the Old Testament enhance your understanding of Jesus as Messiah and his kingdom?

_____

_____

# DAY 4

# The Temple and God with Us

### Read 1 Kings 8:22–61

*"As for the foreigner who does not belong to your people Israel but has come from a distant land because of your name—for they will hear of your great name and your mighty hand and your outstretched arm—when they come and pray toward this temple, then hear from heaven, your dwelling place. Do whatever the foreigner asks of you, so that all the peoples of the earth may know your name and fear you, as do your own people Israel, and may know that this house I have built bears your Name."—1 Kings 8:41–43*

*"And may these words of mine, which I have prayed before the LORD, be near to the LORD our God day and night, that he may uphold the cause of his servant and the cause of his people Israel according to each day's need, so that all the peoples of the earth may know that the LORD is God and that there is no other. And may your hearts be fully committed to the LORD our God, to live by his decrees and obey his commands, as at this time."—1 Kings 8:59–61*

> **Core Truth:** The Creator God desires to be in relationship with all people; he manifests this truth in the Old Testament by dwelling in the midst of his people in anticipation of the coming of Jesus.

King David desires to build a house for God. Instead of allowing David to build, God grants him a covenant promising perpetual rule for his house. Since the time of Moses, God's presence abided in the tabernacle (Exod. 40:34–38). The tabernacle moved about various sites in ancient Israel. During David's reign, he brings the tabernacle to a permanent location on Mount Zion in his new capital city of Jerusalem (2 Sam. 6).

David's son, King Solomon, is responsible for the construction of the temple. First Kings 6–8 narrates its construction. First Kings 8 describes the dedication of the temple. At the heart of the dedication is a prayer by Solomon (8:22–61). Its contents are critical for understanding the function and meaning of the Jerusalem temple.

## Temple Cannot Contain God in All of His Fullness

Just as God's awesome presence filled the tabernacle in the wilderness, it filled the temple on Mount Zion in Jerusalem. This signifies the enthronement of the true King at the center of God's people. The God who first encountered Moses on Mount Sinai now reigns from the temple in Jerusalem. This declaration, however, does not limit God's reign to Israel. The LORD is the king of all creation. God cannot be contained by any part of creation; he rules from outside of it. Solomon recognizes this reality: "The heavens, even the highest heaven, cannot contain you. How much less this temple I have built!" (8:27).

Yet God has chosen to manifest his glory in the midst of his missional people. The vision of Sinai for God's people to serve the nations as a kingdom of priests and a holy nation becomes a reality with the temple in Jerusalem. God's people serve as mediators to the nation of his character and power.

In the New Testament age, God's presence does not physically root in a temple. Following the life, death, and resurrection of Jesus, God's Holy Spirit will reside in each follower of Jesus. Each Christ-follower is a temple (1 Cor. 6:19). Each member of God's people reflects God's character both individually and corporately to the world (Rom. 12:1–2).

## Temple as a Place of Forgiveness and Mercy

The temple is a house of prayer. Profoundly, the temple is a sanctuary for finding forgiveness and mercy. Large sections of Solomon's prayer of dedication anticipate the missteps and future sins of God's people (8:31–40, 44–53). Yet Solomon recognizes that the LORD is a God who forgives and extends mercy to his people. The temple then is a symbol of God's reign and power, but it is also a bold witness to God's love.

God is not a power-hungry despot who rules from on high waiting to punish people when they fail. Many in our world think of God this way. The witness of the temple is that God is *for people,* not only in their triumphs, but also in their failings. This does not mean that God desires his people to fail. Rather it testifies to a different God from all other gods. The LORD is good, just, righteous, forgiving, and loving (Exod. 34:6–7). The temple instills a profound hope that there is always a way forward. The God of the Scriptures is not merely God when things go well; he is God even when the storms of life descend and when we fail to live as the people he created us to be. In those times, God's presence remains, and God invites us to pray and receive his forgiveness and restoration. This is good news.

## Temple and God's Mission

This good news also extends beyond God's people to all the nations. From the time of Abraham, God's people existed to extend God's blessings to all peoples (Gen. 12:3; Exod. 19:4–6). God is not for his people *against* the nations; God is for his people *for the sake* of the nations. God gave his people the land of Canaan and then placed his presence in the temple in Jerusalem as part of his mission to redeem all humanity and heal creation.

The temple serves as a focal point of hope not merely for God's people but for all nations. It witnesses to the world the reality and presence of the true King of all creation. The temple thus is a refuge for the nations. Solomon recognizes the importance of the temple for God's mission explicitly in two places. In 8:41–43, he asks God to hear the prayers of the nations who come to Jerusalem "so that all the peoples of the earth may know your name and fear you, as do your own people Israel, and may know that this house I have built bears your Name" (v. 43). He concludes his dedication with another reminder of God's mission: "so that all peoples of the earth may know that the LORD is God and that there is no other" (8:60).

## Temple and the New Testament

In chapter 6, we talked about the connections between the tabernacle and the coming of Jesus. In the New Testament, Jesus fulfills the role and function of the temple in his person. He brings the presence of God near to all through his life, death, and resurrection. At the moment of his death, the veil concealing the holiest inner room of the temple ("the holy of holies") tears in two (see Matt. 27:51). This signifies the new accessibility of God through the mission of Jesus. Now God abides with his people eternally through the ongoing presence of the Risen Jesus with the church and the indwelling of the Spirit in all who believe. All of this is for the glory of God!

## Questions for Reflection

How have you experienced the forgiveness and mercy of the creator God, who desires salvation for all of his creation?

\_\_\_\_\_

\_\_\_\_\_

Who in your circle of friends and neighbors needs to know the God whom the Bible reveals?

\_\_\_\_\_

\_\_\_\_\_

How well does your community of faith reflect and embody the reality of God's love for the world?

\_\_\_\_\_

\_\_\_\_\_

# DAY 5

# Sin, Exile, and Restoration

Read 2 Kings 17:7–23; 25:27–30; Jeremiah 29:4–23;
Ezra 6:1–18

*In the thirty-seventh year of the exile of Jehoiachin king of Judah, in the year Awel-Marduk became king of Babylon, he released Jehoiachin king of Judah from prison. He did this on the twenty-seventh day of the twelfth month. He spoke kindly to him and gave him a seat of honor higher than those of the other kings who were with him in Babylon. So Jehoiachin put aside his prison clothes and for the rest of his life ate regularly at the king's table. Day by day the king gave Jehoiachin a regular allowance as long as he lived.—2 Kings 25:27–30*

> **Core Truth:** Israel's story serves to encourage us to live faithfully for the mission of the gracious and merciful God who loves us.

In 587 BC, God's people experience a devastating tragedy. The Babylonian Empire under King Nebuchadnezzar ends the reign of David's sons and destroys Jerusalem, including the temple. The Babylonians also force the leading families of God's people to live in exile in Babylon as a means of erasing them from history.

## Causes of Exile

The Bible is clear that the exile occurs because of the unfaithfulness of God's people. It is not the mere might of the Babylonian Empire. God's people continually follow the idolatrous practices of the nations and do not maintain justice for all in their lives with others. In short, they fail in their love for God and neighbor. In the next chapter, we'll see that God sent prophets to call his people back to faithfulness, but they failed to listen to them. Given the longevity of God's people in the land, despite their failings from the period of the judges forward, it is a testimony to God's patience and kindness that exile did not happen sooner.

## Promise of Return

Yet exile was not the end of God's people. The good news for God's people is that there is always a way back due to God's grace and mercy. Already in the book of Deuteronomy, God had promised this: "Even if you have been banished to the most distant land under the heavens, from there the LORD your God will gather you and bring you back" (30:4). The prophet Jeremiah wrote God's people a letter calling them to faithfulness in anticipation of a return to their homeland (29:4–23). God's promises to David also served as a cause for hope (2 Sam. 7:11–16). God's people prayed and longed for a new Son of David to reclaim his throne. Second Kings 25:27–30 is a marker of this hope. It records a remarkable event in 550 BC (thirty-seven years into the exile). Babylonian King Awel-Marduk releases Jehoiachin, the former king of Judah, from prison and gives him a seat of honor at his table. This is significant because Jehoiachin is a son of David and *alive* after almost a generation of exile. If God has sustained a son of David in prison for decades, does this not suggest that the hope for a good future for God's people remains?

## Return and Restoration

Deliverance from exile arrives through the hands of the Persian Empire. The Persians, under Cyrus, defeat the Babylonians and their empire in 539 BC. In 538 BC, Cyrus allows God's people to return to Canaan under the leadership of Zerubbabel (a son of David) and Joshua, the priest (Ezra 1–4). They immediately begin to rebuild the temple. This work is vigorously opposed by the people living around Jerusalem and stalls before completing the temple. Zerubbabel and Joshua exit from the story, but the work of restoration continues. Under the encouragement of the prophets Haggai and Zechariah, the temple is rebuilt and rededicated (521–516 BC).

God raises up Ezra and Nehemiah to lead a spiritual and cultural revival for his newly returned people. They inspire God's people to faithfulness and watch over the rebuilding of Jerusalem and regular celebration of Passover.

This ends the core narrative of God's people in the Old Testament. They have returned to the Promised Land, but full deliverance awaits the coming of the Messiah Jesus in the New Testament.

## Failure and Faithfulness

Reading through Israel's history can be frustrating if we are expecting God's people to always succeed. There are high points, such as Joshua's generation and the early years of King David, but much of the biblical narrative remembers the failings of God's people to live faithfully. The failure of God's people in the Old Testament serves as a warning about the necessity of our own faithfulness. In 1 Corinthians 10:1–13, Paul uses Israel's history as an exhortation to holiness. In 1 Corinthians 10:6, he writes: "Now these things occurred as examples to keep us from setting our hearts on evil things as they did."

Israel's failure to keep covenant with God also serves as an opportunity for God to demonstrate his grace and kindness. God remains faithful to his promises and advances his saving work even when his people stumble. This is not a license for human sin, but rather it is a testimony to the love of God for all creation and to his desire to restore brokenness and offer a new day on the other side of judgment and darkness.

## Waiting in Exile

God's people return to the land, rebuild Jerusalem, and rebuild the temple. But they are no longer free to serve God as a sovereign nation. From 587 BC to the coming of Jesus in the first century AD, God's people live under the authority of the empires of other nations. In succession, the empires of Babylon, Persia, Greece, and Rome rule over God's people. The only exception to this was the Hasmonean Dynasty (142–63 BC) following the Jewish Maccabean revolt against the Greeks. For a brief eighty years, God's people governed themselves, but it was short-lived and the Romans added Palestine to their empire in 63 BC.

Thus, for God's people, exile was over in the sense that they were back in the land with a restored temple, but exile was still a reality because they were not fully free. This created the expectation and hope that God would again fully restore his kingdom by raising up a Son of David to rule (2 Sam. 7).

When Jesus announces the presence of God's kingdom, he is declaring that this future restoration is now. Jesus' life, death, and resurrection are the means by which God restores the kingdom. We now live as witnesses of this hope in anticipation of the full restoration of New Creation.

## Questions for Reflection

How does the story of God's people create hope?

_____

_____


How does it encourage faithfulness in our lives?

_____

_____

# Israel's Life in the Land: The Potential and Pitfalls of Living as God's Missional People

## CORE TRUTHS

1. The courage to listen to Scripture and practice faithfulness are the keys that unlock the future for God's people.
2. Each generation must renew and nurture its relationship with God in order to serve faithfully as God's missional people.
3. God's ideal ruler or Messiah will lead God's people to fulfill his mission by living out faithfully the message of Scripture.
4. The Creator God desires to be in relationship with all people; he manifests this truth in the Old Testament by dwelling in the midst of his people in anticipation of the coming of Jesus.
5. Israel's story serves to encourage us to live faithfully for the mission of the gracious and merciful God who loves us.

## OPEN SESSION WITH PRAYER

## DEBRIEF THE READING FOR THE WEEK (15 MINUTES)

- What were the key takeaways that you gained from this week's reading?
- What aspects of the reading did you find confusing?

- What role does courage play in the life of faith and our fulfillment of God's mission?
- What does Israel's story teach us about the dangers of idolatry?
- What does Israel's story teach us about Jesus and his kingdom?

## WATCH VIDEO (30 MINUTES)

## CONVERSATION (15 MINUTES)

- What aspects of the message resonated with you most deeply?
- What questions did Brian's talk raise for you?
- What would our community look like if it continually realigned itself with Scripture?
- What idols tempt us to turn from God's ways today?
- How well does our community of faith reflect and embody the reality of God's love for the world?
- How does Israel's story inspire hope and faithfulness for us today?

## CLOSING PRAYER

## CHAPTER EIGHT

# The Prophets: Servants of Faithfulness and Proclaimers of God's Future

The writing prophets (Isaiah–Malachi) serve two key purposes in the Bible. First, God sends the prophets to call his people back to their roots as a missional community that exists to extend God's blessings to the nations (Gen. 12:3; cf. Exod. 19:4–6). Second, God's prophets offer a compelling vision of a future act of God that will usher in a new age of salvation and abundance for his people and all creation.

# DAY 1

# Introducing the Prophets

Read 2 Kings 17:7–23

*All this took place because the Israelites had sinned against the Lord their God, who had brought them up out of Egypt from under the power of Pharaoh king of Egypt. They worshiped other gods and followed the practices of the nations the Lord had driven out before them, as well as the practices that the kings of Israel had introduced. The Israelites secretly did things against the Lord their God that were not right. From watchtower to fortified city they built themselves high places in all their towns. They set up sacred stones and Asherah poles on every high hill and under every spreading tree. At every high place they burned incense, as the nations whom the Lord had driven out before them had done. They did wicked things that aroused the Lord's anger. They worshiped idols, though the Lord had said, "You shall not do this." The Lord warned Israel and Judah through all his prophets and seers: "Turn from your evil ways. Observe my commands and decrees, in accordance with the entire Law that I commanded your ancestors to obey and that I delivered to you through my servants the prophets."—2 Kings 17:7-13*

> **Core Truth:** God sent prophets to call God's people to realign with their vocation of serving as God's missional community for the nations.

God's prophets are diverse in origin. Among the writing prophets, Ezekiel is a priest, Isaiah is a political insider, and Amos is a shepherd. While most are men, when we include the narratives about prophets in Joshua–Kings, we will discover that there is a female prophet named Huldah (2 Kings 22:14–20) during the days of Josiah.

God's prophets also deploy both words and physical acts to proclaim God's will for his people. The actual words of the prophets dominate their books, but the prophets use other methods as well. Here are some examples: the book of Jonah speaks God's Word through a narrative about Jonah's mission to the Assyrian city Nineveh. Hosea marries an unfaithful woman for the purposes of illustrating Israel's unfaithfulness to God and his persistent love to woo Israel back to faithfulness.

## Prophets as Forthtellers

The word *prophet* suggests to most people someone who can predict the future, a foreteller. Israel's prophets do point forward to a coming age of salvation, but most of their prophetic words address issues that God's people face in their present context. In other words, God's prophets were primarily *forthtellers* to the present rather than foretellers of the future.

God's prophets speak boldly the very words of God to his people in order to call them to immediate realignment with God's will. God's people preserve the words of the prophets into our biblical books because they have confidence that the Word of God through the prophets will continue to shape the lives of God's people for generations to come. It is crucial for us to learn to read the prophets as authoritative guides for living faithfully as God's people today. If we focus primarily on the future-oriented parts of their words, we distort their message.

## Prophets as God's Response to Unfaithfulness

God sends the prophets in response to the unfaithfulness of God's people. As we've seen in our study of the Bible thus far, God desires for his people to serve as a missional community that reflects God's character in/to/for the nations. Instead, God's people often reflect more the character of the nations by turning to other gods and by participating in social injustice. When God's people lose sight of their true identity, God sends his messengers, the prophets, to deliver a reality check. It is an act of grace that God sends his prophets to call his people to realign themselves with his mission and character.

## The Two Great Threats: Idolatry and Injustice

If the biblical ethos may be summarized succinctly as a call to love God and love neighbor, we can use this rubric to hear the prophetic critique of God's people and the demand for realignment.

It begins with a full allegiance to God. The LORD alone is God. The LORD is the only being deserving of worship. All other "gods" are simply part of creation and need to be submitted to the kingship of God. Yet these other gods constantly tempt God's people and cause their commitment to the LORD to ebb and flow. Living among the nations who did not know the LORD puts God's people in constant contact with other forms of spirituality. God's prophets powerfully call his people back to fidelity to the LORD alone.

In creation, God envisions a harmonious interplay between himself and humanity, but also within humanity and between humanity and the created world. God calls Israel to become a new humanity to serve as ambassadors and witnesses. Israel lives, breathes, and works among the nations but it is to be distinctive and not merely *like* the other nations. Its life together as God's people is to testify to the world about a different kind of God who desires to bless the nations and institute justice, peace, and abundance for all creation.

The ethos of God's people has justice at its center. The call of love for neighbor speaks against special privileges for the powerful and well connected, and extends God's protections and provisions to all, including those most marginalized in society such as slaves, the poor, and aliens.

The Bible steadfastly links spirituality and ethical living. To live as the human beings that God intends for us to be, we have to learn that these elements cannot be compartmentalized. The prophets remind God's people of these truths and insist that one does not love God apart from the practice of justice for others. Moreover, true justice cannot be defined or understood apart from the character of God and faithfulness to him.

## Prophets and Judgment

Reading the prophetic books also challenges the reader about God's coming judgment for unfaithfulness. The prophets are not feel-good preachers. They bring devastating critiques against the unfaithfulness of God's people.

A faithful reading of their words will challenge Christ-followers today to continuous realignment with the mission of God.

## Proclaimers of a New Future

The prophets serve as a natural link to the New Testament. The Old Testament ends with the prophets because they already anticipate a future work of God that will transform God's people and extend God's blessings to the nations. God inspires his people to a profound hope fueled by the anticipation of salvation on the other side of judgment. This salvation would involve the coming of a new King to usher in the kingdom of God and with it transform God's people into the missional community that God would then send into the world to bless the nations.

## Questions for Reflection

What is your understanding of justice?

_____

_____

In what ways do we need to realign in order to love God and love others?

_____

_____

# DAY 2

# Isaiah, Human Lostness, and God's Mission

## Read Isaiah 6:1–8

*In the year that King Uzziah died, I saw the Lord, high and exalted, seated on a throne; and the train of his robe filled the temple. Above him were seraphim, each with six wings: With two wings they covered their faces, with two they covered their feet, and with two they were flying. And they were calling to one another: "Holy, holy, holy is the LORD Almighty; the whole earth is full of his glory." At the sound of their voices the doorposts and thresholds shook and the temple was filled with smoke. "Woe to me!" I cried. "I am ruined! For I am a man of unclean lips, and I live among a people of unclean lips, and my eyes have seen the King, the LORD Almighty." Then one of the seraphim flew to me with a live coal in his hand, which he had taken with tongs from the altar. With it he touched my mouth and said, "See, this has touched your lips; your guilt is taken away and your sin atoned for." Then I heard the voice of the Lord saying, "Whom shall I send? And who will go for us?" And I said, "Here am I. Send me!"—Isaiah 6:1–8*

> **Core Truth:** The prophets remind us that the principal human problem is lostness and alienation due to sinfulness.

The prophets call God's people to realign with his purposes in the world. God calls the prophets in dramatic fashion. Isaiah's call illustrates the key shift that God desires to see in all of his people.

## An Unexpected Encounter

God calls Isaiah during a time of national mourning for the death of King Uzziah in 742 BC. King Uzziah (also known as Azariah in 2 Kings 15:1; cf. 2 Chron. 26:1) reigned for fifty-two years in Jerusalem. He was a good king who led Judah to a time of economic prosperity and peace. Near the end of Uzziah's life, the Assyrian Empire emerged to threaten Judah as well as the entire Near East. The king was dead and presumably so was any hope for the security of God's people.

You can imagine the angst, disappointment, and fear that must fill Isaiah as he journeys to the temple that day. But Isaiah soon learns that neither the death of a king nor the weight of his own fears is his principal problem.

In the midst of the chaos of Isaiah's life stands God—exalted and in control. God's presence is so overpowering for Isaiah that he can only mention God's robe. This doesn't mean Isaiah does not see more, rather it means God's presence is so overwhelming and powerful that Isaiah is unable to say more.

Uzziah had served as Isaiah's security blanket. It is no coincidence that Isaiah encounters the living God as soon as his temporal refuge is removed. Isaiah's encounter with God at precisely the time in which his security had been stripped away suggests that the little kings in our lives have to be removed before we can see the true King.

## Isaiah's Experience of God's Presence

Isaiah is standing in the temple and sees God in all of his glory. Isaiah narrates a full-orbed, multi-sensory encounter with the LORD. Seraphim are circling above God's throne. These heavenly beings function as God's attendants and appear to Isaiah as flames of fire. Unlike God, who remains silent, the seraphim speak.

First, the seraphim affirm, "Holy, holy, holy is the LORD Almighty" (Isa. 6:3). They declare that the LORD is the holiest of all. God is unique. The LORD is exalted over all creation. God's holiness separates him from all created beings and things. God is not found in a rock or in an animal. Humans, the earth, and the vast expanse of space are all finite and part of the creation. Only God is eternal; only God is divine.

Holiness also involves God's character. God is ethically perfect. He sets the standard for what is good.

The seraphim also announce, "The whole earth is full of his glory" (v. 3). The holy God engages his creation. God's glory fills the created world. Glory refers to God's awesome presence. God's presence is not confined to a sanctuary in heaven or on earth. God is involved in our world and cares deeply for those who are lowly and troubled. The psalmist proclaims this good news: "Who is like the LORD our God, the One who sits enthroned on high, who stoops down to look on the heavens and the earth? He raises the poor from the dust and lifts the needy from the ash heap" (Ps. 113:5–7).

## Isaiah's Fundamental Problem

Isaiah recognizes his predicament in the presence of the Holy One. There are no complaints, pleas for help, or prayers. He is finished due to his sin.

In the presence of God, Isaiah learns that his primary problem is not Uzziah's death or the Assyrian army. Isaiah suddenly realizes that *he* is the problem.

God had called Isaiah and all Israel to be a kingdom of priests and a holy nation (Exod. 19:5–6). Instead, Isaiah confesses, "I am a man of unclean lips, and I live among a people of unclean lips." Isaiah went to the temple mourning the death of Uzziah. His cry, "Woe to me!" indicates that he now mourns for himself.

In the presence of God's holiness, we realize that our problem is our sin—our tendency toward self-centeredness and our neglect to do God's will. The good news for Isaiah and for us is that the only One capable of saving us is both willing and able.

## God's Grace

At Isaiah's moment of need, God cleanses him. He is a man of unclean lips before the King of kings. He doesn't plead for forgiveness. But God is gracious nonetheless.

God's grace flows freely to all who recognize their inability to save themselves and their radical need for God's salvation. Isaiah is cleansed by the searing love of God through the seraph's action of touching his mouth with a coal from the altar of burnt offering. In Romans 3:23–24, the apostle Paul so clearly summarizes Isaiah's experience of God's grace: "For all have sinned and fall short of the glory of God, and all are justified by his grace through the redemption that came by Christ Jesus."

## Calling and Mission

As soon as Isaiah has been cleansed, he hears the voice of God for the first time. "Whom shall I send? And who will go for us?" (v. 8).

God's questions remind us that his saving grace is not merely personal. The gospel comes to us on its way to someone else. It is ultimately for the world. God delivers us from our sins so that we can become his agents of blessing to others.

There is no compulsion in the Isaiah story. God does not command Isaiah; he asks. Isaiah responds with some of the most famous words in the Bible: "Here am I. Send me!" (v. 8).

Long ago Isaiah went to his place of worship and met God there. God opened his eyes, cleansed him from sin, and unleashed him for service. This paradigm remains our calling today.

## Questions for Reflection

How does Isaiah's calling and commissioning remind us of the principal problem of our world?

_____

_____

What "kings" in your present life prevent you from seeing and serving the true King?

_____

_____

How would your life be different if you prayed, "Here am I. Send me!"?

_____

_____

# DAY 3

# The Prophetic Call to Practice Justice

Read Amos 2:6–8; 4:1–5; 5:21–24; Micah 6:6–8

*"I hate, I despise your religious festivals; I cannot stand your assemblies. Even though you bring me burnt offerings and grain offerings, I will not accept them. Though you bring choice fellowship offerings, I will have no regard for them. Away with the noise of your songs! I will not listen to the music of your harps. But let justice roll on like a river, righteousness like a never-failing stream!"—Amos 5:21–24*

*With what shall I come before the LORD and bow down before the exalted God? Shall I come before him with burnt offerings, with calves a year old? Will the LORD be pleased with thousands of rams, with ten thousand rivers of olive oil? Shall I offer my firstborn for my transgression, the fruit of my body for the sin of my soul? He has shown all you people what is good. And what does the LORD require of you? To act justly and to love mercy and to walk humbly with your God.—Micah 6:6–8*

---

**Core Truth:** In God's kingdom, justice is central; peace, joy, love, mercy, kindness, and Sabbath rest exist in abundance for all creation.

---

God's prophets proclaim the justice of God. The biblical call for justice is central to the ethos of God's kingdom. The Bible links love for God with love for neighbor. God's people must embody his character in their lives together as well as in their treatment of other people and the creation as a whole. God's call for justice is central to the proclamation of the kingdom. In God's kingdom, there is peace, joy, love, mercy, kindness, and Sabbath for all. There is no room for the status quo values rooted in power, exploitation, class status, and militarism. Part of Israel's witness was its treatment of the marginalized.

During the early eighth century BC, both the northern kingdom (Israel) and the southern kingdom (Judah) enjoyed a time of economic prosperity. Unfortunately, this prosperity did not include all of the people. God sent his prophets, including Amos and Micah, to call his people to realign their lives with the full ethos of Sinai: love for God *and* love for neighbor.

## Misuse of Religious Acts

The Bible refuses to separate our spiritual lives from our moment-by-moment existence in the world. It matters profoundly how God's people live. To love God cannot be isolated from our love for neighbor. This extends even to the integrity of our acts of worship. During Amos' and Micah's day, God's people consistently *practiced* their religion by attending to the required religious sacrifices and festivals. The words of the prophets therefore must have stunned them. In Amos 4:4–5 and 5:21–23, Amos announces God's displeasure with the worship of his people. God's displeasure is so great that Amos writes: "I hate, I despise your religious festivals; I cannot stand your assemblies" (5:21). Micah's words in 6:6–7 are in a similar vein.

The prophets write these words because *external* religious actions alone are insufficient. God wants a whole-being response (Deut. 6:4–5). In Amos' day, some of God's people use religious acts as a means to elevate themselves over others rather than to honor and worship the LORD. In Amos 4:5, he says, "Burn leavened bread as a thank offering and brag about your freewill offerings—boast about them, you Israelites, for this is what you love to do." God's people must avoid the subtle danger of turning an act of devotion to God into an act that brings attention and honor to the worshiper. Worship must center on the adoration of God or it's not worship.

Also *external* religious acts must be practiced in concert with our love for others. Amos and Micah call God's people to account for this error. The gospel involves reconciliation with God and *with others*. The New Testament affirms this perspective. In the Sermon on the Mount, Jesus teaches, "Therefore, if you are offering your gift at the altar and there remember that your brother or sister has something against you, leave your gift there in front of the altar. First go and be reconciled to them; then come and offer your gift" (Matt. 5:23–24). James offers this advice to the outwardly religious: "Religion that God our Father accepts as pure and faultless is this: to look after orphans and widows in their distress and to keep oneself from being polluted by the world" (1:27).

## Abuse of the Poor

When God's people do not protect and bless the poor, his mission becomes compromised. Following Jesus is not a self-help plan for prosperity at the expense of others. Amos champions the cause of the oppressed among God's people. His words call God's people to account for their neglect and abuse of the marginalized. Amos's opening words to God's people (2:6–8) are set within a wider sermon on the sins of the nations. In 1:1–2:5, Amos addresses Israel's neighbors for their abuses of others. This sets up Amos to deliver a knockout blow to God's people themselves. If it is wrong for the nations to oppress and abuse others, how much more wrong is it for *God's people* to participate in these practices? God's people are to serve as a missional community that reflects God's character in/to/for the nations. Holiness matters. When God's people do not embody God's values, they compromise God's mission and their testimony becomes toothless. If our lives do not align with God's values, our witness points away from God rather than to God. In Amos' day, God's people allowed the guilty to abuse the innocent and failed to protect the poor and the needy in the courts and in the marketplace.

## Practicing Justice

Amos, in words that Martin Luther King Jr. made famous, declares, "But let justice roll on like a river, righteousness like a never-failing stream" (5:24). The God who delivered his people from the injustice of Egypt demands that his people create opportunities for all to experience God's abundance. In God, there is hope for the poor, the widow, and the orphan. In his kingdom, God will tear down the proud and lift up the humble. A commitment to justice recognizes the giftedness and sanctity of life and works for a world where all can live as the people God created them to be.

At the end of the day, God wants more than lip service and external acts of worship. God desires to transform us into conduits of kindness and compassion in a world that desperately needs it. The prophet Micah succinctly captures the essence of the missional holiness that God desires for his people to embody: "He has shown all you, O mortal, what is good. And what does the LORD require of you? To act justly and to love mercy and to walk humbly with your God" (6:8).

When God's people model his justice, the world sees a witness to life as he intended for it to be. The New Creation is coming, but in the meantime, God's people offer the world a taste of heaven in the present through their embodiment of justice.

## Questions for Reflection

How would your life, as well as the life of your community of faith, look different if justice were a core value?

_____

_____

Where do you see injustice in the world today?

_____

_____

How would God's mission be enhanced if we manifested God's justice in our homes, workplaces, schools, and neighborhood?

_____

_____

# DAY 4

# God's Mission for the Nations

Read Isaiah 42:1–7; 49:5–6; Jonah 3:10–4:11

*This is what God the Lord says—the Creator of the heavens, who stretches them out, who spreads out the earth with all that springs from it, who gives breath to its people, and life to those who walk on it: "I, the Lord, have called you in righteousness; I will take hold of your hand. I will keep you and will make you to be a covenant for the people and a light for the Gentiles, to open eyes that are blind, to free captives from prison and to release from the dungeon those who sit in darkness."—Isaiah 42:5-7*

---

**Core Truth:** The prophets remind God's people that God desires to extend his salvation to all nations.

---

God's people are a missional community. God calls Israel to be a blessing for the nations. God sends his prophets to call his people to realign with God's mission. This means turning from idolatry and injustice to embrace faithfulness. But faithfulness is ultimately the means for living as God's missional people. The prophets thus remind God's people of the role that they play for the nations.

## Isaiah 40–55 and the Nations

In Isaiah 40–55, the prophet reminds God's people of their mission to the nations. This section of Isaiah focuses on God's servant as the agent of his mission (Isa. 42:1–7; 49:1–6; 50:4–9; 53; cf. Isa. 61:1–3). The first two of these emphasize the servant's role of establishing justice as well as extending blessing to the nations. The next section will reflect on the role of the suffering servant to enact God's abundant future.

Isaiah 42:4–7 sets the servant's work in the context of God's global mission. Since Genesis 3–11, God has been working to redeem all of humanity through the calling of his people. Due to the lack of faithfulness among God's people, he is now at work redeeming them from exile, but the full mission to all humanity remains in view. God's servant will establish justice not only for God's people, but on earth as a whole (42:4). The servant will renew God's people and be a "light for the Gentiles" (42:6). This tension between God's work on behalf of his people and of the nations is crucial for understanding how to read Scripture. All readers of Scripture must listen for its call to realignment. Scripture calls God's people to realign while simultaneously inviting the nations to align with its good news. The servant embodies this dual focus. The servant works to restore God's people while extending God's blessings to the wider world.

Isaiah 49:5–6 continues this theme. Verse 6 is crucial for understanding the servant's mission, the role of God's people, and God's desire to extend salvation to all creation: "It is too small a thing for you to be my servant to restore the tribes of Jacob and bring back those of Israel I have kept. I will also make you a light for the Gentiles, that my salvation may reach to the ends of the earth." The full implication of God's desire to reach the nations comes to light in the book of Jonah.

## Jonah and God's Love for the World

The prophet Jonah reminds God's people that he loves the whole world, including the enemies of God's people. The gospel is hope for all.

God calls the prophet Jonah to go to Nineveh, the capital of the feared Assyrian Empire. Jonah flees from this call and ends up being delivered by God from a raging storm by means of a large fish (Jon. 1–2).

Jonah 3:1 opens up in identical fashion as 1:1, with God renewing his call for Jonah to travel to Nineveh and proclaim his message to the Ninevites. This time Jonah goes. Nineveh is an exceedingly great city. This emphasizes the missional need of Nineveh. In 1:2, its wickedness is noted. Here its vastness takes center stage because it demonstrates their great need for good news.

Jonah announces the impending destruction of Nineveh in forty days. The Ninevites from great to small respond in repentance to the LORD by putting on sackcloth and sitting in ashes. Even the mighty king of Nineveh reacts. He orders a fast, a time of prayer to God, and a turning from all evil—even the animals of Nineveh are covered in sackcloth. Jonah witnesses the full repentance of Nineveh. Unlike his initial response to God's call, the Ninevites respond wholeheartedly to the word of God. This is a powerful word for God's people about how even enemies and those far from God's ways can respond positively to the good news.

The hated and feared Ninevites have repented fully and put their hope in God's mercy. How would God respond? God saw the repentance of the Ninevites (3:10) and relents from the judgment that he planned. He does not destroy Nineveh. This is exceedingly good news for Nineveh but also for all outsiders. God is gracious to more than his own people. God's people exist for the sake of the lost world of Genesis 3–11. The extent of God's love for the world will be fully revealed in the life, death, and resurrection of Jesus, but it is already present here. If God can relent of his judgment on the wicked Ninevites, is anyone beyond the reach of his love?

This may be really good news for Nineveh and, by implication, all outsiders, but Jonah is greatly displeased. In 4:2, we learn the true reason that Jonah fled from the LORD. He was not afraid of the Ninevites. Instead, Jonah fled out of fear that God might show compassion to the Ninevites. This is precisely what occurred! In 4:2, Jonah quotes the LORD's self-affirmation of his love and compassion from Exodus 34:6–7. On Sinai, after Israel turned from God to the golden calf, God showed himself to be a God of limitless love and compassion. Jonah understood this, but he did not like that God might love his enemies with this same compassion. This is the danger for insiders. We forget that God loves our enemies. In fact, we forget that the reason for our existence as God's people is so that outsiders can have the opportunity to become insiders. Jonah is so displeased with God's mercy to the Ninevites that he asks God to take his life rather than having to witness the sparing of Nineveh from the wrath of God. In the last verse (4:11), God reminds us of his heart for *all creation*: "And should I not have concern for the great city Nineveh, in which there are more than a hundred and twenty thousand people who cannot tell their right hand from their left—and also many animals?"

## Questions for Reflection

How would our lives change if we embraced God's vision of the world?

_____

_____

How would we view those we perceive as "enemies" or "others"?

_____

_____

Who, specifically, is our mission?

_____

_____

# DAY 5

# The Prophets and God's Coming New Age of Salvation

Read Isaiah 53; 56:3–8; 61:1–3; Jeremiah 31:31–34; Ezekiel 36:26–27; Joel 2:28–32

*"The days are coming," declares the LORD, "when I will make a new covenant with the people of Israel and with the people of Judah. It will not be like the covenant I made with their ancestors when I took them by the hand to lead them out of Egypt, because they broke my covenant, though I was a husband to them," declares the LORD. "This is the covenant I will make with the people of Israel after that time," declares the LORD. "I will put my law in their minds and write it on their hearts. I will be their God, and they will be my people. No longer will they teach their neighbor, or say to one another, 'Know the LORD,' because they will all know me, from the least of them to the greatest," declares the LORD. "For I will forgive their wickedness and will remember their sins no more."—Jeremiah 31:31–34*

---

**Core Truth:** The prophets boldly announce a hope-filled future new age of salvation ushered in by a new king who will secure God's victory.

---

The prophets call God's people back to their roots. But they also look forward to a future age of abundance when God will do a great work of salvation. This vision offers hope to God's people. We will focus on Jeremiah 31:31–34 and supplement his vision with others from the prophets to paint a picture of the hope that they announce to God's people.

## Hope on the Other Side of the Tragedy of Exile

In 587 BC, exile in Babylon began for God's people. Even after their return from captivity in 538 BC, God's people still languished under the oppressive rule of foreign powers.

Jeremiah's remarkable words in 31:31–34 announce a new day when God's people would experience a shift in their life with God. God would offer a new covenant to replace the old Sinai covenant. The old covenant had been broken repeatedly by the unfaithfulness of God's people. God remains faithful as he always does. So Jeremiah speaks a bold word about a coming new covenant to create hope for God's people. Jeremiah's words announce boldly that God's work of salvation is not merely in the past. The God who delivered his people from Egypt remains committed to fulfilling his mission to bring hope, healing, and restoration to the world. This is the good news of the prophets. While they offer devastating critiques of the unfaithfulness of God's people, they always point to a good future on the other side of judgment.

## Hope for Transformation

The future that Jeremiah envisions begins with a life-altering encounter with the living God. The story of God's people is a habitual pattern of unfaithfulness. God recognizes this problem and vows to do a new work to make it possible for his people to live faithfully. Jeremiah foresees God doing a work on the *inside of people*. When God's new covenant arrives, God will *internalize* the law on the hearts and minds of his people.

Instead of struggling to be faithful, God's people will be unleashed to live lives of *faithful obedience* through personal transformation. The power to live for God will bubble forth from *inside* of God's people. It will permeate into all areas of life so that God's people will truly live as the people of God for the world. Ezekiel saw this as God exchanging hard and rebellious hearts for hearts open to the moving of God. The prophet Joel declared that God's Spirit would be the central figure in making this a reality for all of God's people (2:28). In the New Testament, God will pour out the Holy Spirit to cleanse his people and empower them to live fully for God.

## Hope for Personal Relationship with God

Jeremiah envisions a new age of personal relationship with God. Don't misread this as a call for individualism over community. God calls us to be a missional community, but such a community grows out of individuals joining together around their experience of God. Jeremiah foresees a day when each of God's people will truly *know the* LORD. This intimacy contrasts with mere knowledge *about* God or with emphasizing *religious* acts over the deep spirituality of a moment-by-moment walk with God.

God's desire for personal relationships with men and women has its roots in the Garden of Eden, where humanity and God enjoyed daily fellowship. Men and women who know the LORD are a people ready for mission. By knowing the LORD, we become clues that point others to God.

## Hope for a Missional Community

Jeremiah's vision includes a renewed people of God as a whole. God's people form a corporate witness to the truth of God. Yet an individual approach to faith remains a temptation for God's people. We must remember that an individualistic faith is foreign to biblical faith, including the new future described by Jeremiah. The prophet can clearly envision a new community of God's people drawn "from the least of them to the greatest" (Jer. 31:34).

The danger of a self-referential faith is that it exists for the individual rather than for the world. The same danger exists for communities isolated from the world. Just as God freed Israel from Egypt to function as a priestly kingdom and a holy nation for the sake of all nations, so also in the new covenant, God's people corporately function as a missionary people: "But you are a chosen people, a royal priesthood, a holy nation, God's special possession, that you may declare the praises of him who called you out of darkness into his wonderful light" (1 Pet. 2:9).

## Hope for a New King

Israel's future hope centers on the return of a son of David to rule over God's kingdom. Isaiah shows that the coming messianic figure will achieve God's victory through suffering. Isaiah 53 describes the sacrificial death of God's servant as the means of purifying his people and advancing his mission. The servant dies for the pain, suffering, and sin of God's people (53:4–6, 12). The New Testament recognizes this as a description of the life, death, and resurrection of Jesus (e.g., Acts 8:26–40).

Isaiah 61:1–3 offers a slightly different portrait. Here Isaiah speaks of God's Spirit-anointed ruler. He will usher in God's kingdom by announcing the arrival of his age of abundance where the brokenhearted are made whole, prisoners find liberation, the poor hear the good news, and the year of God's favor arrives. This is the fullest expression of the suffering servant of Isaiah 53. Isaiah is describing God's kingdom. So when Jesus announces the kingdom of God (Matt. 4:17; Mark 1:15), he declares that God's future is now a reality. As we move into the New Testament, the hope of the prophets finds its fulfillment in the gospel of Jesus Christ.

## Questions for Reflection

What role does hope play in your understanding of spirituality?

\
\

How does the Bible's vision of hope differ from the way the world talks about hope?

\
\

How does knowing that God's future will be an abundant one inspire you to live faithfully for God's mission today?

\
\

# The Prophets: Servants of Faithfulness and Proclaimers of God's Future

## CORE TRUTHS

1. God sent prophets to call God's people to realign with their vocation of serving as God's missional community for the nations.
2. The prophets remind us that the principal human problem is lostness and alienation due to sinfulness.
3. In God's kingdom, justice is central; peace, joy, love, mercy, kindness, and Sabbath rest exist in abundance for all creation.
4. The prophets remind God's people that God desires to extend his salvation to all nations.
5. The prophets boldly announce a hope-filled future new age of salvation ushered in by a new king who will secure God's victory.

## OPEN SESSION WITH PRAYER

## DEBRIEF THE READING FOR THE WEEK (15 MINUTES)

- What were the key takeaways that you gained from this week's reading?
- What aspects of the reading did you find confusing?
- What role do the prophets play in Israel's story?
- How does Isaiah's calling and commissioning remind us of the principal problem of our world?

- How do the prophets remind Israel of their vocation as a missional community?
- How did the prophets envision the future?

## WATCH VIDEO (30 MINUTES)

## CONVERSATION (15 MINUTES)

- What aspects of the message resonated with you most deeply?
- What questions did Brian's talk raise for you?
- In what ways do we need to realign in order to love God and love others?
- How would your life, as well as the life of your community of faith, look different if justice were a core value?
- What role does hope serve in the life of faith?
- How does knowing that God's future will be an abundant one inspire us to live faithfully for God's mission today?

## CLOSING PRAYER

## CHAPTER NINE

# Jesus, the Church, and God's Mission

The Old Testament presents act 1 of God's story: creation, the fall, and Israel. We discovered the world as God intended, our world as marred by sin and human lostness, and God's calling of a missional people to reflect his character in/to/for the world. Act 1 ended with Israel back in its land following exile and with the expectations of a new king and new era of salvation. Jesus' coming marks the beginning of act 2: Jesus, the church, and new creation. This is the story of the New Testament.

We have added a sixth day of study for this chapter in order to do full justice to the message of Jesus.

# DAY 1

# Jesus Fulfills the Old Testament Story

Read Psalm 22; Matthew 1:1; 5:17–48;
1 Corinthians 15:3–5

*"Do not think that I have come to abolish the Law or the Prophets; I have not come to abolish them but to fulfill them. For truly I tell you, until heaven and earth disappear, not the smallest letter, not the least stroke of a pen, will by any means disappear from the Law until everything is accomplished. Therefore anyone who sets aside one of the least of these commands and teaches others accordingly will be called least in the kingdom of heaven, but whoever practices and teaches these commands will be called great in the kingdom of heaven. For I tell you that unless your righteousness surpasses that of the Pharisees and the teachers of the law, you will certainly not enter the kingdom of heaven."—Matthew 5:17–20*

---

**Core Truth:** The life, death, and resurrection of Jesus reenact and fulfill the Old Testament story.

---

Jesus is God's agent to bring salvation to a lost humanity and heal a broken world. The New Testament seeks to announce the gospel of Jesus—his life, death, and resurrection—as the fullest expression of Israel's story. The story line that began with creation, the fall, and Israel reaches its climax in Jesus the Messiah.

## Jesus: Creation and the Fall

Jesus fulfills the potential of humanity. Jesus comes to model the ideal human life. He serves God's mission by announcing God's kingdom. He creates a new community and expands God's people's understanding of community. He embodies the character of God to the world. In other words, Jesus lives out the story that Adam and Eve and every subsequent human were supposed to live.

Jesus' sacrificial death on the cross makes it possible for us to be human again. Jesus dies to demonstrate decisively and definitively God's power, desire, and ability to save. Jesus dies for our sins so that we can live. Jesus dies so that condemnation, death, injustice, fear, pain, suffering, shame, darkness, alienation, depression, deprivation, humiliation, brokenness, and all of the other challenges and afflictions that result from the effects of the fall of humanity will not have the final word. God's final word to humanity and all creation is life. This is the good news.

## Jesus and the New Israel

Jesus' life retells Israel's story. As we read the New Testament, we will find quotations and references to the Old Testament on virtually every page. The biblical authors make it clear that the life, death, and resurrection of Jesus brings the Old Testament story and God's promises to a climax.

In the Gospels, Jesus' ministry follows the preaching of John the Baptist. The Gospels present John as the last of the Old Testament prophets who arrives to prepare the way the coming of the Messiah. Jesus' birth stories (Matthew 1–2 and Luke 1–2) present Jesus as the fulfillment of Old Testament prophetic expectations.

## Jesus and the Kingdom

Jesus begins his ministry by proclaiming God's kingdom. This kingdom is the fulfillment of the promised new future (new covenant/new heart/new king) envisioned and proclaimed by Israel's prophets. Jesus understands his words and actions as a declaration of the arrival of God's future age of salvation into the present. In Luke 4:16–21, we encounter the remarkable story of Jesus standing up in his hometown synagogue and reading from Isaiah 61:1–2: "The Spirit of the Lord is on me, because he has anointed me to proclaim good news to the poor. He has sent me to proclaim freedom for the prisoners and recovery of sight for the blind, to set the oppressed free, to proclaim the year of the Lord's favor" (Luke 4:18–19). Kingdom language in Jesus' day captures the expectations and hopes embedded in the words of the prophets.

Jesus also creates a new Israel by calling twelve disciples to himself. These twelve disciples mirror the twelve tribes of Old Testament Israel. The community Jesus launches becomes a new Israel, which exists to bless the nations by proclaiming and embodying the kingdom in imitation of Jesus the Messiah. Jesus leads this missional community and trains them to extend God's blessings in/to/for the nations.

Jesus teaches the fullest meaning of the Mosaic covenant (Matt. 5:17–20). Jesus embraces love as the overarching theme for understanding the ethos of God's people (Matt. 5:43–48). Jesus' ethic involves holding together the twin commandments: love God and love neighbor. Jesus teaches and embodies an expanded vision of neighbor. He challenges our tendency to limit love to those closest and most like us. He lifts up the model of God the Father who "causes his sun to rise on the evil and the good, and sends rain on the righteous and the unrighteous" (Matt. 5:45). Jesus works to eliminate barriers that prevent outsiders from experiencing God's salvation through the work of God's people.

## Jesus as Israel's Messiah

Jesus fulfills the messianic expectations of the Old Testament. The New Testament refers to him as Jesus *Christ* or *Messiah*. Christ means Messiah. This is Jewish language for the return of God's anointed king to deliver his people from oppression and lead them in his mission. The ideal Israelite king was the appointed agent through whom God administered his kingdom. The promises to David (2 Sam. 7) served to raise the expectation of a renewal of kingship. Thus, it is significant that Jesus is linked genealogically with the lineage of David (Matt. 1:1–17 and Luke 3:23). Moreover, the crowds often acknowledged Jesus as Son of David.

The final week of Jesus' life begins with his dramatic entry into Jerusalem riding a donkey. This act is bold and daring because through it Jesus symbolically announces his identity as Messiah. Israel's Scriptures had foretold of the return of Messiah to Jerusalem upon a donkey (Zech. 9:9–10).

## Jesus' Death and Resurrection

The events of Jesus' crucifixion unfold in fulfillment of the Old Testament. Jesus gathers with his disciples on the night of his betrayal to eat the Passover meal. Jesus' death occurs precisely when God's people were remembering the exodus. Jesus' death and resurrection announce a new liberation for all the earth. On the cross, God defeats all sin, death, suffering, and shame. Jesus dies embodying the words of Psalm 22. Jesus quotes verse 1, "My God, my God, why have you forsaken me?" While Jesus suffers, other events from Psalm 22 unfold around him including the insults of those watching, soldiers gambling for his clothes, and water pouring out of his side. The psalm ends with the hope of vindication (22:22–31). By quoting Psalm 22, Jesus demonstrates his identification with the suffering psalmist, but also anticipates his deliverance in the resurrection.

From birth to resurrection, Jesus' life reenacts the Old Testament story.

## Questions for Reflection

How did your study of the Old Testament expand or change your prior understanding of Jesus?

_____

_____

How does Jesus' living out of the Old Testament Scriptures give us a model of a life shaped by Scripture?

_____

_____

# DAY 2

# The Kingdom and Breaking Down Boundaries

### Read Matthew 8:1–17

*When Jesus had entered Capernaum, a centurion came to him, asking for help. "Lord," he said, "my servant lies at home paralyzed, suffering terribly." Jesus said to him, "Shall I come and heal him?" The centurion replied, "Lord, I do not deserve to have you come under my roof. But just say the word, and my servant will be healed. For I myself am a man under authority, with soldiers under me. I tell this one, 'Go,' and he goes; and that one, 'Come,' and he comes. I say to my servant, 'Do this,' and he does it." When Jesus heard this, he was amazed and said to those following him, "Truly I tell you, I have not found anyone in Israel with such great faith. I say to you that many will come from the east and the west, and will take their places at the feast with Abraham, Isaac and Jacob in the kingdom of heaven. But the subjects of the kingdom will be thrown outside, into the darkness, where there will be weeping and gnashing of teeth." Then Jesus said to the centurion, "Go! Let it be done just as you believed it would." And his servant was healed at that very hour.—Matthew 8:5–13*

---

**Core Truth:** Jesus' kingdom challenges God's people to reach out to those outside the community so that they may become insiders and followers of Jesus.

---

Jesus' life, death, and resurrection demonstrate decisively that the kingdom of God has arrived. As we saw in chapter 1, Jesus came to announce and unleash the kingdom of God into our present age. One of the key teachings of Jesus is the necessity of moving past the boundaries that separate God's people from those who God desires to bless with the good news. Followers of Jesus must navigate the tension of living for God while living in the world. Religion has a tendency to build walls. In our day, religion often hardens into political and ideological commitments that stand in opposition to the very kingdom that we seek to follow. Yet God's mission is to redeem humanity—*all humanity*. This includes even persons that stand on the *outside* of our comfort zones. For God's mission to advance, God's people cannot establish impermeable boundaries. By his actions, Jesus offers an exemplary example of cutting through the inherited prejudiced and suffocating status quo that often plagues humanity.

## The Kingdom and Boundary-Breaking

In Matthew's gospel, Matthew has skillfully constructed chapters 8–9 as a report of the mighty acts of Jesus. The initial segment (8:1–17) is instructive for seeing Jesus' kingdom-signifying actions regarding the shattering of religious and cultural boundaries. Jesus performs three explicit miracles in this segment: the cleansing of a leper (8:1–4), the healing of a centurion's servant (8:5–13), and the healing of Peter's mother-in-law (8:14–15).

Why does Matthew report these three healings in this order? All three of the persons whom Jesus engages in his healing actions represent a group marginalized in some fashion by the pious circles of first-century Judaism. They are all outsiders to the good news of the kingdom. The leper is ritually unclean. Due to his skin ailment, he cannot worship or even mingle with his community. Instead, religious regulations mandate that he live on the fringes of society as an unwanted outcast. The Roman centurion represents the hated empire and is a tangible reminder of the ongoing exiled condition of God's people even in their own land. Likewise, the healing of Peter's mother-in-law is significant because women enjoy much lower status than men in the culture of the time. It is significant then that Jesus' initial miracles involve persons from these marginalized groups.

The importance of breaking boundaries is central to the values of the kingdom. The gospel is for *all humanity*. Moreover, the gospel advances through its introduction to *outsiders*. When former *outsiders* become *followers of Jesus*, they become new guides of God's grace to previously unreached people. Jesus' boundary-breaking creates a new *mission*-driven people. Transformed people are compelling conduits of the gospel from the moment of their conversion.

Reflect on the three groups mentioned in Matthew 8 (lepers, foreigners, and women). All of these groups become surprising witnesses for the power of the gospel. Jesus sends the leper immediately to the priest to serve as "a testimony to them" (8:4). The centurion is praised for his great faith (8:10–11). In Mark's gospel, the centurions present at the crucifixion become the first public proclaimers of Jesus' true identity, "Surely this man was the Son of God!" (Mark 15:39). This is profound in that their confession mirrors Peter's earlier declaration at Caesarea Philippi (Matt. 16:16). But unlike Peter—who balked at the understanding of Jesus as Son of God and his death on a cross (Matt. 16:21–23; Mark 8:33)—the centurions recognize the reality of Jesus' identity after watching how he died. In essence, they are the first truly public witnesses of Jesus and they are outsiders. Likewise, women will serve as the initial witnesses of Jesus' resurrection (Matt. 28:1–10; cf. Mark 16:1–8; Luke 24:1–12; John 20:1–18). Deploying women as heralds of the good news of God's victory is profoundly significant and subversive. Women are unable to serve as witnesses in legal disputes, yet God unleashes them to be the first proclaimers of the resurrection. Their message ultimately changed the world.

## Boundary-Breaking Today

The very act of boundary-breaking demonstrates the reality of the kingdom that Jesus announces at the beginning of his ministry (Matt. 4:17; Mark 1:13–15; Luke 4). Jesus desires to shape us into a missional community that reflects God's character in/to/for the world. The gospel comes to us on its way to someone else.

Thus, by engaging such *outsiders* actively and without reservation, Jesus models a cross-cultural and boundary-exploding mission that can run against the current of societal prejudice and injustice. There will always be *outsiders* who are seeking the opportunity to become *insiders and followers of Jesus.* The gospel is liberating and egalitarian in outlook. God's mission involves extending the message of the kingdom to all people, especially to those marginalized by society or by religious insiders. Boundary-breaking mission also keeps social justice on the front burner. Jesus demonstrates through his life that God is radically for the marginalized, the poor, the sick, the dying, the foreigner (even representatives of the *privileged* empire), and the outcast. Christ-followers of today would do well to heed this model as they plot to launch to communities of faith. Where would Jesus establish new communities of faith today? What people in our immediate proximity and neighborhood represent *outsiders*? What would it look like for our community to extend the good news of the gospel beyond those like us? Reading the Gospels reminds us that a biblical model of missional outreach will always include persons *different* from us.

## Questions for Reflection

What does a community open to all look like?

_____

_____

Who are people excluded from our communities today?

_____

_____

What challenges does an inclusive community have to face?

_____

_____

How does Jesus' boundary-breaking call us to change?

_____

_____

# DAY 3

# The Kingdom and Lostness

Read Luke 15:1–32

*"When he came to his senses, he said, 'How many of my father's hired servants have food to spare, and here I am starving to death! I will set out and go back to my father and say to him: Father, I have sinned against heaven and against you. I am no longer worthy to be called your son; make me like one of your hired servants.' So he got up and went to his father. But while he was still a long way off, his father saw him and was filled with compassion for him; he ran to his son, threw his arms around him and kissed him. The son said to him, 'Father, I have sinned against heaven and against you. I am no longer worthy to be called your son.' But the father said to his servants, 'Quick! Bring the best robe and put it on him. Put a ring on his finger and sandals on his feet. Bring the fattened calf and kill it. Let's have a feast and celebrate. For this son of mine was dead and is alive again; he was lost and is found.' So they began to celebrate."—Luke 15:17–24*

---

**Core Truth:** God's mission is driven by God's extraordinary and extravagant love for all humanity.

---

Jesus' story about a lost or prodigal son in Luke 15:11–32 challenges us to embrace the fullness of God's love for the world. It teaches us the extraordinary love of God the Father for all humanity.

## Lost Things

Luke 15 includes three stories about lostness: a lost sheep (vv. 3–7); a lost coin (vv. 8–10); and a lost son (vv. 11–32). Religious leaders criticize Jesus for engaging tax collectors and sinners; such persons were the lost and damned.

Good religious people didn't associate with them. Jesus demonstrates that the kingdom's good news is good news even for the lost. This truth presents a jarring reality to the religious insiders. But it offers hope of God's abundance for those deemed lost.

Jesus begins with two stories to draw his hearers in. First, a person with one hundred sheep loses one and leaves the ninety-nine to find it. Jesus knows that his audience will approve and relate with celebrating the lost sheep's recovery. Jesus then adds the takeaway: "I tell you that in the same way there will be more rejoicing in heaven over one sinner who repents than over ninety-nine righteous persons who do not need to repent" (v. 7).

Second, Jesus immediately launches into another similar story. The math changes a little. A woman with ten coins loses one. Jesus assumes that his audience will identify with the woman's obsession with finding the lost coin and the joy that she experiences upon finding it. Again Jesus ends with a broader implication: "In the same way, I tell you, there is rejoicing in the presence of the angels of God over one sinner who repents" (v. 10).

## A Lost Son

Jesus jumps into the story of a lost son. The math shrinks again—first one hundred sheep, then ten coins, and now two sons. The younger son stunningly dishonors his father by requesting his inheritance before his father's death. In any culture, this is inappropriate, but within the first-century context and given that the son is the youngest, it is profoundly offensive. The audience would expect the father at minimum to react negatively and perhaps even disown this shameful son. But the father does the unexpected. He divides his property between his two sons.

The younger son leaves home and squanders his entire inheritance on wild living. He finds himself impoverished and on the verge of starvation. As a Jew, he suffers the shame of caring for ceremonially unclean pigs. Yet he is so hungry that he longs to eat pigs' food. Insight arrives when he realizes that the hired servants of his father live better than he does.

He returns home to confess his sins to his father and asks to be made a servant. This is a risky move because he has already dishonored his father by asking for the money. Then he wasted it in a foreign land and shamefully returns home empty-handed. This is a further dishonor to his father.

Stunningly, the father spies his lost son on the road leading to the family estate, is filled with compassion, runs to his son, and kisses him! In the culture of the Mediterranean world, this action was jaw-dropping. Fathers didn't do this to even a good son, let alone the very son who dishonored and humiliated him with his shameful request, immoral living, and empty-handed return home. But Jesus is not talking about any father; Jesus is describing the attitude and actions of God the Father toward lost people.

## Celebrating Being Found

The father in Jesus' story celebrates with an extravagant party. The father clothes the returning son in splendor and orders the preparation of the fattened calf. But Jesus adds a plot twist. The eldest son is not so happy over the celebration. He does not share the joy of his father. In fact, he is angry and refuses to enter the home. By not entering the home and joining the celebration, he now dishonors his father.

The father responds in the same way as he did with the younger son. The father chooses the opportunity to love extravagantly rather than react to being dishonored. The father goes to the son rather than waiting for the son to come to him. The elder son spews a list of complaints and even compares himself to a slave. The father calmly reminds the elder son of his blessed position. The celebration is no slight to the elder son; rather it is an opportunity for rejoicing because a lost member of the family has been restored. At this point the story ends. Does the elder son join the party? Who is the lost son at the end of the story? We as readers must decide.

## Lostness and Mission

Luke 15 models perfectly the missional heart of God. There is a powerful word both to the insider and outsider. To both, there is an explicit call to realign with the values of the kingdom as modeled by the Father's heart. To the religious insider (in this context, the complaining Pharisees and teachers of the law), these stories of lostness challenge them to realign with God's true mission of extending his blessings to lost people whom they are excluding by their customs. To the outsider (tax collectors and sinners), these stories stress that God is radically for them and longs to celebrate their entrance into the community of faith. These stories serve as invitations. God himself is a shepherd who leaves the ninety-nine to find the one. God is the woman who earnestly looks for the lost coin. God is the father who goes against the customs of preserving self-honor and extends extravagant love and compassion to both of his lost sons.

The gospel always comes to us on its way to someone else. As Dr. Robert Tuttle suggested, we need to pray for the father's heart: "Lord, help me to love others as though they were my own children. Amen."[9]

## Questions for Reflection

What is keeping you from returning to the God who loves you?

_____

_____

How do these stories of God's extravagant love for lost people challenge your present attitude about people who are different than you?

_____

_____

How do we need to change as a community of faith to reach out to outsiders?

_____

_____

Do we rejoice as God rejoices when a lost person receives mercy, love, and compassion?

_____

_____

# DAY 4

# Responding to the Kingdom: Belief and Unbelief

### Read Matthew 13:1–9, 18–23, 44–46

*That same day Jesus went out of the house and sat by the lake. Such large crowds gathered around him that he got into a boat and sat in it, while all the people stood on the shore. Then he told them many things in parables, saying: "A farmer went out to sow his seed. As he was scattering the seed, some fell along the path, and the birds came and ate it up. Some fell on rocky places, where it did not have much soil. It sprang up quickly, because the soil was shallow. But when the sun came up, the plants were scorched, and they withered because they had no root. Other seed fell among thorns, which grew up and choked the plants. Still other seed fell on good soil, where it produced a crop—a hundred, sixty or thirty times what was sown. Whoever has ears, let them hear."—Matthew 13:1-9*

---

**Core Truth:** God calls his people to be sowers of the Word and vigilant in faithfulness.

---

Part of the scandal of the gospel is the reality of unbelief. Jesus announces the kingdom and makes its transformational power evident and available to all who encounter him. Likewise, as followers of Jesus, we work to embody the values and ethics of the kingdom and share its good news for the world. Sometimes followers of Jesus can become discouraged that their efforts bear little fruit or signs of success.

## The Parable of the Sower

In Matthew 13:1–9, Jesus tells a parable, or story, that serves as a paradigm for understanding the role of God's people in the world and how the kingdom of God expands. Jesus draws on the common agricultural practices of his day to communicate an important message for his disciples. In 13:18–23, Jesus interprets his own parable for the disciples. Jesus describes a farmer who goes out to sow seeds. This is pre-modern farming so there are no tools or machines. There are not even nice neat rows. In the ancient world, the farmer simply scattered seeds on the field indiscriminately. The ancient farmer had little control over the outcome of his work. All seeds had the potential for growth, but their ultimate production hinged on the *type* of soil present where they landed.

In Jesus' story, there are four types of soil. First, some seed falls on the pathways that border the farmer's plot. Birds on the lookout for an easy meal gobble these up long before they have the chance to grow. Other seed falls on rocky soil. It germinates quickly but withers just as fast because it cannot develop deep roots. Still other seed falls among thorns. It also germinates and begins to grow, but the thorns choke the plants before they can produce fruit. Yet some seed lands on good soil. These produce an abundant crop that more than makes up for the unfruitful seeds.

Jesus explains that this is a parable about the word of the kingdom and its reception by people. First, it is a word of encouragement to God's people that they must remain persistent and vigilant in widely and indiscriminately declaring the good news of the kingdom. The encouragement comes in the reminder that God's people are not responsible for the growth of the kingdom. This parable emphasizes that it is the soil that counts. If the word lands on a receptive person, there is the opportunity for an abundant harvest. If the word lands on poor soil, the same word produces nothing. God's people are thus free from the tyranny of results. They simply proclaim the good news faithfully with the understanding that it will take root in some.

## Reasons for the Lack of Belief

The parable also explores reasons for unbelief. By using the poor soils to illustrate why people may prove to be unreceptive to the gospel, Jesus' words remind God's people of the hazards and costs of discipleship. Jesus focuses on three areas: the actions of the evil one, persecution and trouble caused by aligning oneself to Jesus' kingdom, and the allures of life and wealth.

Jesus affirms the reality of Satan as the personification of evil and enemy of faith. The New Testament never lifts up Satan as the cause of every evil. In his kingdom, Jesus defeats Satan through the casting out of demons and by teaching his disciples to pray for "deliverance from the evil one" (Matt. 6:13). But Jesus' words remind us that Satan remains the enemy of faith and desires nothing more than to squash faith before it has time to germinate.

The two middle soils share something with the fruitful soil. The seeds planted in them begin to grow. But due to the soil, the plants are unable to produce fruit. In the case of the rocky soil, the cause is persecution and hardships. Following Jesus can be risky and costly. Families may disown converts. Christ-followers may lose jobs and business contacts. During the first century, Christians faced persecution from Rome and from competing religious groups. Even today, Christ-followers may find themselves threatened with death, imprisonment, or physical harm. For some, this pressure is too much and they lose the ability to be fruitful. Their faith withers.

For most of us reading this, the gravest threat is the danger posed by the wealth and opportunities of our world. The desire for affluence and prosperity threaten to choke the possibilities of the kingdom. Following Jesus is an *all-in* proposition (Matt. 16:24). The danger of affluence is the subtle temptation to trade in the life and mission of the kingdom for comfort, pleasure, and security. Sometimes we try to combine these with the gospel, but as Jesus warns, the desire for wealth threatens to choke out our ability to bear fruit for the kingdom.

## An Abundant Harvest

Jesus' words end with an assurance that the kingdom will bear fruit. Yes, few may receive the message of the kingdom, but the faithful must not lose heart because the harvest that will come from the few will be abundant. Harvests of thirty, sixty, and a hundred-fold all represent plentiful amounts well above the expectations of the farmer.

It is important to recognize the possibility of sliding between soils. The life of faith is a moment-by-moment one. New challenges and possibilities arise with each day. If we desire to follow Jesus, we must be vigilant in guarding our hearts and minds lest we become unfruitful. Otherwise the mission is "Keep sowing!"

## Questions for Reflection

With what soil do you identify?

_____

_____

What is the greatest threat to your ability to be fruitful—the evil one, persecution, or the allures of affluence?

_____

_____

How well do you persist in sowing seeds to those in your life?

_____

_____

To whom is God calling you to sow seeds today?

_____

_____

# DAY 5

# Living "All In" for
# Jesus' Kingdom

### Read Matthew 16:21–28

*From that time on Jesus began to explain to his disciples that he must go to Jerusalem and suffer many things at the hands of the elders, the chief priests and the teachers of the law, and that he must be killed and on the third day be raised to life. Peter took him aside and began to rebuke him. "Never, Lord!" he said. "This shall never happen to you!" Jesus turned and said to Peter, "Get behind me, Satan! You are a stumbling block to me; you do not have in mind the concerns of God, but merely human concerns." Then Jesus said to his disciples, "Whoever wants to be my disciple must deny themselves and take up their cross and follow me. For whoever wants to save their life will lose it, but whoever loses their life for me will find it. What good will it be for someone to gain the whole world, yet forfeit their soul? Or what can anyone give in exchange for their soul? For the Son of Man is going to come in his Father's glory with his angels, and then he will reward everyone according to what they have done. Truly I tell you, some who are standing here will not taste death before they see the Son of Man coming in his kingdom."—Matthew 16:21-28*

> **Core Truth:** Jesus calls his followers to live for his kingdom by offering themselves fully to God and following Jesus into the world on mission.

Following Jesus is a bold calling. Jesus describes the essence of being his disciple in Matthew 16:24. In response to a challenge by Peter, Jesus says, "Whoever wants to be my disciple must deny themselves and take up their cross and follow me."

## Peter's Rebuke

Jesus defines discipleship because Peter challenges his mission. In 16:21, Jesus informs his disciples that he will travel to Jerusalem where he will suffer, be killed, and be raised on the third day. This baffled his disciples because it conflicted with their expectations of the Messiah. Peter rebukes Jesus for speaking of suffering and death. In fact, he does it emphatically, "This shall never happen to you!" (v. 22); Jesus responds strongly, "Get behind me, Satan!" (v. 23). Jesus does not mean that the devil has possessed Peter. By his words and desires Peter is aligning himself with evil. For indeed, Jesus' mission involves laying down his life sacrificially for the world.

## The Dangers of Discipleship

According to Jesus, Peter's problem is his focus on "merely human concerns" rather than "the concerns of God" (v. 23). Peter has lost sight of God's mission and he values human matters above it. What does this mean? First, focusing on human concerns means valuing security and personal peace over God's plan. Jesus is going to Jerusalem to suffer and die. Peter prefers to avoid this fate. Later he will deny Jesus rather than risk his life. True security is found in God alone (Matt. 16:27–28). The future of the disciple is secure. Claims of security in this age are an illusion and ultimately a hindrance to living the unbelievable life that God calls us to live on behalf of his kingdom.

Second, Peter values a different type of messiah. A crucified messiah is not in Peter's plans. Death on a cross is shameful. Peter desires a messiah who would triumph through worldly means.

## A Radical Cross-Centered Life

At the heart of Jesus' call in Matthew 16:24 is a simple truth: live your life as though you were already dead.

First, following Jesus involves self-denial. When we talk of self-denial, we reduce it to giving up chocolate or TV for a time. This may be a good spiritual practice, but it is not radical enough. God wants us to be all in for his kingdom. The word translated "deny" is the same word used to describe Peter's threefold denial of Jesus. In these cases, Peter is seeking to save himself by denying or renouncing any relationship with Jesus. To deny oneself, then, is renouncing one's claim to self-preservation.

Second, following Jesus means identifying with the way of the cross. To take up one's cross is best illustrated when Roman soldiers force Simon of Cyrene (Matt. 27:32) to take up Jesus' cross and bear it to the place of Jesus' execution. This shows the literal meaning of the phrase. To "take up one's cross" is to live as though you were on the final journey of your life. To use a modern phrase, it is to live as a "dead man walking." Jesus calls his followers to a radical life in which they die to themselves up front and then paradoxically find life. Listen to his words in Matthew 16:25, "For whoever wants to save their life will lose it, but whoever loses their life for me will find it."

Last, once we have embraced the cross, we follow Jesus moment by moment. Where does Jesus lead us? Jesus leads us into the world on mission to announce the good news of the kingdom to those most desperate for it.

## A Secure Future

Jesus is not calling persons merely to die for a lost cause. It is not about intentional martyrdom. Jesus' call is radical, but it is rooted in a secure future. Jesus was going to Jerusalem to die, but he anticipated resurrection (16:21). Resurrection would follow suffering and death. We live with the boldness of the dead because our future is absolutely secure. In Matthew 16:27–28, Jesus says, "For the Son of Man is going to come in his Father's glory with his angels, and then he will reward each person according to what they have done. Truly I tell you, some who are standing here will not taste death before they see the Son of Man coming in his kingdom."

These verses point to an abundant future. The future is secure so we can live bravely and boldly for Jesus in the present. The way of Jesus Christ is about life in the kingdom (present and future). This is a hope that ought to unleash us to live fully for God in the present.

## Jesus' Call to Us

As we reflect on Jesus' call to discipleship, we realize that Jesus is calling us to die to ourselves and our self-interests so that we can truly live. We must ask ourselves as individuals: *Am I all in for God's mission?* I am to live as one who is carrying my own cross—a person with nothing left to lose. There is great freedom in this. In other words, the focus can no longer be on self at all, but on Jesus Christ. And when we focus on Jesus Christ, we must inevitably face the cross. At the cross, we find the essence of discipleship. At the cross, God invites us to live as a community of the cross. At the cross, God receives us with open arms. We are no longer lost sons and daughters of Adam and Eve. God shapes us into a mosaic of formerly broken pieces that are now renewed and transformed by the cross so that we can offer wholeness, hope, and salvation to a broken world. We join with others to live as a missional community that exists to embody and reflect God's values and character in/to/for the world.

## Questions for Reflection

How would your life be different if you fully embraced the way of Jesus?

_____

_____

What in your current life is keeping you from the way of the cross?

_____

_____

Are you all in?

_____

_____

# DAY 6

# Cross, Resurrection, and Mission

Read Matthew 26:17–30; 27:32–56; 28:1–20;
Romans 5:1–11

*Then the eleven disciples went to Galilee, to the mountain where Jesus had told them to go. When they saw him, they worshiped him; but some doubted. Then Jesus came to them and said, "All authority in heaven and on earth has been given to me. Therefore go and make disciples of all nations, baptizing them in the name of the Father and of the Son and of the Holy Spirit, and teaching them to obey everything I have commanded you. And surely I am with you always, to the very end of the age."—Matthew 28:16–20*

---

**Core Truth:** Jesus' death and resurrection achieves God's ultimate victory over sin, brokenness, and injustice and opens an abundant future for all who trust in him.

---

The story of Jesus reaches its climax in his death and resurrection. His death demonstrates God's love for the world (Rom. 5:8) and decisively deals with human sin and injustice by opening up an abundant future for all who trust in him.

## The Scandal of the Cross

All four Gospels record the dramatic end of Jesus' earthly life. The combined forces of Rome, the religious leadership, and the crowds all conspire to send

Jesus to a brutal death on a cross. The message is clear: all humanity is responsible for the death of Jesus. Crucifixion was a form of capital punishment reserved for slaves and rebels against Rome. It did not bring death swiftly but instead prolonged the suffering and shame of the one being executed. For a Jew, it was scandalous because it involved the shame of being hung on a tree. To the Romans, it marked a violent and humiliating end to a life in a way that stripped its victim of any status and crushed all hope. Paul will later write, "For the message of the cross is foolishness to those who are perishing, but to us who are being saved it is the power of God" (1 Cor. 1:18).

## The Meaning of the Cross

Jesus' death was purposeful. Jesus willingly laid down his own life for the world. The Gospels offer complementary reflections on the meanings of his death. John describes Jesus' death as the fullest expression of love: "Greater love has no one than this: to lay down one's life for one's friends" (John 15:13). God loved all humanity enough to give his Son for their benefit (John 3:16).

Matthew, Mark, and Luke reflect on the meaning of Jesus' sacrifice by describing the initial celebration of the Lord's Supper. Jesus offers bread and wine as symbols of his death. Matthew 26:28 reads, "This is my blood of the covenant, which is poured out for many for the forgiveness of sins." These words indicate decisively that Jesus' death is an act *for us*. Jesus' death is *for our sins*. Jesus emphasizes the importance of covenant between God's people and God at the Last Supper when he says, "This cup is the new covenant in my blood, which is poured out for you" (Luke 22:20). Jesus' death establishes the new covenant promised in the prophets and a clear pathway to God.

Last, Jesus' death is also for the evils and injustices of the world. In Matthew 8:17, Matthew comments that Jesus healed the sick and cast out demons in fulfillment of Isaiah 53:4: "He took up our pain and bore our suffering." Isaiah 53:4–6 is central to the early church's preaching on the cross (see Acts 8:30–35). Typically Isaiah 53 is used to proclaim Jesus' death for sin, but Matthew reminds us that Jesus died also for pain, suffering, demonic oppression, and affliction. Jesus' saving death is God's answer to all sin and evil post Genesis 3–11.

## Resurrection, New Life, and God's Mission

Jesus' death did not mark the end of Jesus the Messiah. God raised him from the dead to definitively announce the victory of love over all darkness and sin. God saves us through the life, death, and resurrection of Jesus.

Jesus' resurrection becomes the impulse for a new stage in the mission of God. Jesus unleashes his disciples to carry the gospel to the ends of the earth. It is news that must be shared. The first heralds of the resurrection are the women who found the tomb empty on the third day. The angel sends them to announce Jesus' resurrection to the disciples. In the first century, women were not allowed to testify in a court of law because they were considered unreliable. Yet, God entrusts them with the message of resurrection. This is a crucial word for us today. We may not always feel ready or qualified, but God has given us a story to testify and embody. The news of Jesus' resurrection is the most important news in history *and* God entrusts it to a group of faithful women. He entrusts it to us, too.

Next, Jesus appears to his remaining eleven disciples (Matt. 28:16–20). He commissions them to *make disciples of all nations*. Jesus moved throughout the land of Israel in fulfillment of the Old Testament's vision of Messiah. Now post-resurrection, he sends his followers into the *whole* world in fulfillment of God's mission to *bless the nations*. "Go" becomes the church's mantra. With the resurrection of Jesus, God's people now become both a sending and a sent community. The *movement* that Jesus models becomes the modus operandi for the church.

Post-resurrection, the biblical story opens up fully to the nations. The scope of God's mission becomes explicitly for *all nations*. The entire world of Genesis 1–11 is the target of the gospel. In the Old Testament, Israel's mission was one of *being* and *living* as a kingdom of priests and a holy nation. With few exceptions (e.g., Jonah) the nations had to come to Israel to learn about God. Now there is a grand reversal. Jesus' disciples "Go and disciple" (Matt. 28:18–20) by engaging all peoples with the gospel.

## God with Us

Profoundly Jesus is called Immanuel ("God with us") at his birth. It is fitting that the Gospel of Matthew ends with the fullest expression of this promise.

After commissioning his followers to carry the good news to the world, Jesus ends with a promise: "And surely I am with you always, to the very end of the age" (v. 20). Don't miss this. The risen Christ, Immanuel, leads his people as they embody his humanity-and-creation-loving kingdom in/to/for the world. Let's go.

## Questions for Reflection

What does Jesus' death and resurrection mean for your life and mission?

_____

_____

What does it mean to "make disciples"?

_____

_____

How does Jesus fulfill the biblical theme of "God with us"?

_____

_____

# Jesus, the Church, and God's Mission

## CORE TRUTHS

1. The life, death, and resurrection of Jesus reenact and fulfill the Old Testament story.
2. Jesus' kingdom challenges God's people to reach out to those outside the community so that they may become insiders and followers of Jesus.
3. God's mission is driven by God's extraordinary and extravagant love for all humanity.
4. God calls his people to be sowers of the Word and vigilant in faithfulness.
5. Jesus calls his followers to live for his kingdom by offering themselves fully to God and following Jesus into the world on mission.
6. Jesus' death and resurrection achieves God's ultimate victory over sin, brokenness, and injustice and opens an abundant future for all who trust in him.

## OPEN SESSION WITH PRAYER

## DEBRIEF THE READING FOR THE WEEK (15 MINUTES)

- What were the key takeaways that you gained from this week's reading?
- What aspects of the reading did you find confusing?
- How do the life, death, and resurrection of Jesus fulfill the Old Testament?

- What do the presentation of Jesus and kingdom teach us about God and mission?
- What do Jesus' death and resurrection mean for our lives and mission?

## WATCH VIDEO (30 MINUTES)

## CONVERSATION (15 MINUTES)

- What aspects of the message resonated with you most deeply?
- What questions did Brian's talk raise for you?
- What boundaries need to be broken in our communities?
- How do we need to change as a community of faith to reach out to outsiders?
- What is the greatest threat to your ability to be fruitful—the evil one, persecution, or the allures of affluence?
- What does it mean for us to be all in for the kingdom?
- Who is our mission?

## CLOSING PRAYER

## CHAPTER TEN

# Church and New Creation

Post-resurrection Jesus appears to his disciples and sends them in the power of the Holy Spirit to carry the good news of the kingdom to all people. The church serves as God's new Israel made up of Jews and Gentiles in fulfillment of God's mission to bring salvation to the lost world of Genesis 3–11. The New Testament story traces the movement of the gospel by Jesus' apostles such as Paul to the Roman Empire. The church advances courageously because it is grounded in an audacious hope that God's abundant future of love and justice is absolutely secure. Living in anticipation of this New Creation, God's people proclaim the good news and start new communities of faith all over the Roman world.

# DAY 1

# Mission and the Holy Spirit

Read Joel 2:28–32; Acts 1:8; 2:1–41; 28:30–31

*When the day of Pentecost came, they were all together in one place. Suddenly a sound like the blowing of a violent wind came from heaven and filled the whole house where they were sitting. They saw what seemed to be tongues of fire that separated and came to rest on each of them. All of them were filled with the Holy Spirit and began to speak in other tongues as the Spirit enabled them. Now there were staying in Jerusalem God-fearing Jews from every nation under heaven. When they heard this sound, a crowd came together in bewilderment, because each one heard their own language being spoken. Utterly amazed, they asked: "Aren't all these who are speaking Galileans? Then how is it that each of us hears them in our native language?"—Acts 2:1–8*

---

**Core Truth:** The Holy Spirit empowers God's people to carry the good news of the gospel to all people.

---

The book of Acts demonstrates the empowering role of the Holy Spirit in the advancement of the gospel. It opens with the risen Jesus preparing his disciples for the post-resurrection mission. Jesus' words are powerful: "But you will receive power when the Holy Spirit comes on you; and you will be my witnesses in Jerusalem, and in all Judea and Samaria, and to the ends of the earth" (1:8).

## The Church and Genesis 3–11

With the coming of the Holy Spirit, God's people reengage the Genesis 3–11 world—the biblical story from Abraham (Gen. 12), through the life and ministry of Jesus centered on Israel as God's new missional people. Now post-resurrection, God sends this new humanity into all of the world. To follow Jesus is to go.

Acts 1:8 begins God's mission locally where Jesus served—Jerusalem and the wider land of biblical Israel. But now there is a movement toward the rest of the world. The gospel reached its initial fulfillment in the land of Israel. Now it must spread to the nations. The biblical story line reconnects with God's universal mission to all creation. God had originally intended for creation to be filled with image-bearing women and men who reflected his character (Gen. 1:26–31). In the power of the Spirit, God's new humanity—the church—embodies this mission.

## Empowered by the Holy Spirit

The Spirit is the driver of God's mission in the world. After Jesus' resurrection, God sends the Spirit to unleash his people to serve as witnesses to the good news of the kingdom. The empowerment of the Spirit is the key difference between the Old and New Testament people of God. The church is a people of the Spirit.

Acts 2 narrates the Spirit's dramatic arrival on the Day of Pentecost. Devout Jews, as well as Jewish converts from all over the world, gather in Jerusalem. On the morning of Pentecost, Jesus' followers gather in prayer. Suddenly the Holy Spirit arrives on them in the form of tongues of fire. The Spirit enables each Christ-follower (perhaps as many as one hundred twenty; cf. 1:15) to speak one of the native languages of those visiting Jerusalem. This reality reverses the confusion of Babel (Gen. 11:1–9) and shows that the gospel was for all languages and ethnic groups. God wants to reach and speak into every human culture. Peter announces to the crowd that this miracle of speech is the fulfillment of the prophecy from Joel 2:28–32. God's future age of the Spirit has now come. Peter's Spirit-empowered preaching adds three thousand new believers.

## The Holy Spirit and the Growth of God's People

In Acts, each advance of the gospel is marked by new baptisms of the Spirit. In the Old Testament, only select individuals were filled with the Spirit, but in the

New Testament, all of God's people receive the Spirit. Acts records the apostles performing miracles and preaching in the power of the Spirit. Whenever the gospel reaches a new area, the Spirit fills the believers there.

The Spirit propels the gospel forward. In Acts 3, Peter heals a lame man and boldly proclaims the gospel in Solomon's portico. After Peter and John are arrested in Acts 4, the Spirit fills Peter (4:8) and enables him to share a powerful word before the council.

In Acts 7–8, the church comes under intense persecution. Ironically, the persecution serves to advance the gospel by pushing it out of Jerusalem into surrounding regions. Persecution does not mark the end of witness, but is often a conduit for increasing the effectiveness of Christian witness. The persecution in Jerusalem causes Jesus' followers to scatter and the gospel arrives in new places. It comes first to Samaria (7:4–25) under the work of Philip. When reports of the conversions of Samaritans arrive back at Jerusalem, the apostles send out Peter and John to investigate and resource the new community of faith. When they arrive, they pray for the Spirit to come upon the new believers in Samaria (7:15–17) and it does. The Spirit's arrival marks the gospel's coming. The same happens when the gospel impacts Gentiles in Caesaria (10:44–48). This outpouring of the Spirit marks God's acceptance of new believers into the kingdom regardless of whether they are Jew (Acts 2), Samaritan (Acts 7), or Gentile (Acts 10). This is a further fulfillment of Joel's vision of the Spirit being poured out on "all flesh" (Joel 2:28). The gift of the Spirit is for all God's people.

The Spirit is the guiding force in the gospel's advance from Jerusalem in Acts 1 to Rome in Acts 28. It provides guidance for God's people. In Acts 8:26–40, the Spirit prompts Philip (8:29) to engage an Ethiopian eunuch in a conversation that leads to conversion. The Spirit fills Saul (Paul) in 9:17 after the risen Jesus meets him on the road to Damascus (9:1–9). The Spirit transforms Paul from a persecutor of the church to a leading apostle.

## Rome and Beyond

Acts 13–28 narrates the movement of the gospel from Jerusalem to Rome. Acts 13:1–4 credits the Spirit with the advance of the gospel. The Holy Spirit commissions and sends out Paul (Saul) and Barnabas to preach the gospel in these new lands. Paul and Barnabas ultimately separate (Acts 15:36–41) but Paul continues his missional work. Under the guidance of the Spirit (16:6–10),

MISSION AND THE HOLY SPIRIT

Paul leaves Asia for Macedonia and Greece. The gospel continues to move forward until Acts ends in chapter 28 with Paul preaching about Jesus in Rome itself. The story ends abruptly. The implication is clear. Since there is no Acts 29, we are left to dream under the Spirit's influence about the chapters that the Spirit will write with our lives.

## Questions for Reflection

Describe the role of the Holy Spirit in the advance of the gospel.

_____

_____

What story do you sense that God desires to write through your life?

_____

_____

Who is your mission?

_____

_____

# DAY 2

# The Apostle Paul
# and God's Mission

Read Romans 1:14–17; 3:21–31; 8:18–23;
2 Corinthians 5:16–6:2

*I am obligated both to Greeks and non-Greeks, both to the wise and the foolish. That is why I am so eager to preach the gospel also to you who are in Rome. For I am not ashamed of the gospel, because it is the power of God that brings salvation to everyone who believes: first to the Jew, then to the Gentile. For in the gospel the righteousness of God is revealed—a righteousness that is by faith from first to last, just as it is written: "The righteous will live by faith."—Romans 1:14–17*

---

**Core Truth:** Paul proclaims a gospel that reconciles humanity and all creation through the life, death, and resurrection of Jesus.

---

Paul's life dominates the book of Acts. The New Testament includes thirteen of his letters. The heart of Paul's gospel was reconciliation. Paul powerfully proclaimed a reconciliation with God that demolished the walls that separated humanity from God, others, and the created world.

## Reconciliation with God

Paul's gospel centers on the death and resurrection of Jesus the Messiah. In 1 Corinthians 15:3–4, Paul shares the testimony he received at his conversion, "Christ died for our sins according to the Scriptures, that he was buried, that he was raised on the third day according to the Scriptures." Jesus' death and resurrection demonstrate God's love (Rom. 5:8) and reconcile the world to God.

230

Paul captures this in 2 Corinthians 5:19, "that God was reconciling the world to himself in Christ, not counting people's sins against them." Reconciliation is by faith (Rom. 1:16). Reconciliation with God makes it possible for us to live fully as the people whom God created us to be.

Paul proclaims Jesus' death and resurrection as God's victory for all creation. The gospel calls God's people to realign their understanding of mission and invites outsiders to reconciliation with God. God's people have a mission. It began with the creation of humanity (Gen. 1:26–31). Reconciliation with God serves as a commission to mission. We become Jesus' ambassadors. Paul writes, "We are therefore Christ's ambassadors, as though God were making his appeal through us. We implore you on Christ's behalf: Be reconciled to God" (2 Cor. 5:20).

## Reconciliation of Humanity

Paul's gospel expands our vision of God's people. It is no longer Israel and everyone else. If the Old Testament from Genesis 12–Malachi focuses on Israel in anticipation of Messiah, Paul articulates an expansive vision for God's new Israel, the church. Membership in God's people does not require Gentiles becoming Jews. Paul writes: "I am obligated both to Greeks and non-Greeks, both to the wise and the foolish. That is why I am so eager to preach the gospel also to you who are in Rome. For I am not ashamed of the gospel, because it is the power of God that brings salvation to everyone who believes: first to the Jew, then to the Gentile" (Rom. 1:14–16). Paul even includes those people ("barbarians") viewed by the Greco–Roman world as outsiders and inferior people groups. For Paul there is no "them" only "us." In Ephesians 2:13–14, Paul writes further of the reconciliation of Jews and Gentiles, "But now in Christ Jesus you who were once far away have been brought near by the blood of Christ. For he himself is our peace, who has made the two groups one and has destroyed the barrier, the dividing wall of hostility." There is only one humanity *in Jesus the Messiah*. We reach our fullest humanity in Jesus.

*In Jesus the Messiah,* all divisions end: ethnicity, status, and sex. Paul writes, "There is neither Jew nor Gentile, neither slave nor free, nor is there male and female, for you are all one in Christ Jesus" (Gal. 3:28). The gospel subverts all distinctions that separate people. Paul is not denying diversity. The gospel declares a unity in the Messiah that embraces all and forges a beautiful mosaic that reflects God's vision of a new humanity. Unity is found in Jesus and his mission in the world. Paul envisions God's people as the body of the Messiah in which each member is free through the power of the Holy Spirit to serve in God's mission.

In our world, God's people must work for reconciliation between groups. The gospel subverts all human attempts, and even inclinations, toward separation. Loving God and loving neighbor includes working for authentic reconciliation on the human level as a tangible witness to the reality of God's victory in Jesus the Messiah. The knocking down of bridges dividing humanity looks to God's future in which God and his mission are praised: "And they sang a new song, saying: 'You are worthy to take the scroll and to open its seals, because you were slain, and with your blood you purchased for God persons from every tribe and language and people and nation. You have made them to be a kingdom and priests to serve our God, and they will reign on the earth'" (Rev. 5:9–10).

## Reconciliation with Creation

God's work in Messiah Jesus also enables the reconciliation of the created world. Humanity's original mission was to serve as stewards of God's creation. This is still humanity's mission, but after Genesis 3–11, God's focus is the salvation of humanity so that men and women may live out his creational purposes. God's mission requires a redeemed humanity. Yet Paul reminds us of the gospel's implications for all creation. The gospel announces the nearness of the full redemption of all creation:

> I consider that our present sufferings are not worth comparing with the glory that will be revealed in us. For the creation waits in eager expectation for the children of God to be revealed. For the creation was subjected to frustration, not by its own choice, but by the will of the one who subjected it, in hope that the creation itself will be liberated from its bondage to decay and brought into the freedom and glory of the children of God. We know that the whole creation has been groaning as in the pains of childbirth right up to the present time. Not only so, but we ourselves, who have the firstfruits of the Spirit, groan inwardly as we wait eagerly for our adoption to sonship, the redemption of our bodies. (Rom. 8:18–23)

There is mystery here, but Paul's vision of the gospel includes the full salvation of all creation.

In sum, Paul recognizes that the gospel makes possible a reconciliation that heals the disastrous effects of the fall (Gen. 3–11). The life, death, and resurrection of Jesus the Messiah make this possible. As Paul writes in 2 Corinthians 5:17, "Therefore, if anyone is in Christ, the new creation has come: The old has gone, the new is here!"

## Questions for Reflection

What does it mean to serve as Jesus' ambassador?

_____

_____

How does the gospel bring reconciliation to humanity and all creation?

_____

_____

Are you ready to experience reconciliation with God and join Jesus in his mission?

_____

_____

# DAY 3

# Sharing the Good News
# with All People

Read Acts 17:10–33; 1 Corinthians 9:19–22

*Though I am free and belong to no one, I have made myself a slave to everyone, to win as many as possible. To the Jews I became like a Jew, to win the Jews. To those under the law I became like one under the law (though I myself am not under the law), so as to win those under the law. To those not having the law I became like one not having the law (though I am not free from God's law but am under Christ's law), so as to win those not having the law. To the weak I became weak, to win the weak. I have become all things to all people so that by all possible means I might save some.—1 Corinthians 9:19–22*

> **Core Truth:** The gospel calls all of God's people to engage in acts of witness to the surrounding world.

In the life, death, and resurrection of Jesus, God has ushered in a new age of salvation in which all nations are fully welcomed. Paul's calling was the proclamation of this gospel across the Roman world to both Jew and Gentile. Paul embodies his role as apostle by carrying the gospel to new cities and regions in the Greco-Roman world. Paul profoundly understands the "go-to" ethos that the people of God must embody in the age of the church (Matt. 28:18–20; Acts 1:8). Paul's self-understanding involves a commitment to preach the gospel in areas that have not yet heard of the Messiah Jesus. Paul grasps the necessity of making Jesus known across the world as the fulfillment of God's mission. When writing to the Christians in Rome of his anticipated visit to them, he pens these remarkable words:

It has always been my ambition to preach the gospel where Christ was not known, so that I would not be building on someone else's foundation. Rather, as it is written: "Those who were not told about him will see, and those who have not heard will understand." This is why I have often been hindered from coming to you. But now that there is no more place for me to work in these regions, and since I have been longing for many years to visit you, I plan to do so when I go to Spain. I hope to see you while passing through and to have you assist me on my journey there, after I have enjoyed your company for a while. (Rom. 15:20–24)

Paul's words are not arrogant. He is not writing as some lone-ranger evangelist who wants sole credit for the number of converts. It is clear from his writings that Paul worked closely with many other Christ-followers, including Timothy, Barnabas, Aquila, Priscilla, and Epaphroditus among others. Paul also recognizes that God is ultimately responsible for growing the church and that this mission is advanced by everyone playing his part in God's grand drama (1 Cor. 3:5–9).

Rather, Paul's words in Romans 15 are astonishingly audacious and a crucial reminder of the necessity of continuously advancing the gospel beyond its current status quo. Reflect for a moment about Paul's desire to preach where Christ was not yet known. During Paul's ministry (AD 40s–early 60s), followers of Jesus were a tiny minority. The churches of the New Testament were small house-churches. From reading Paul's letters, it is clear that Paul knew many of the earliest Christians personally. Thus when he talks of taking the gospel to a new place, we must remember that he is not talking about waiting for the gospel to saturate an area before carrying it to another. He is talking about spreading the gospel widely and continually. Paul models the "go-to" ethos of the New Testament. His work as an apostle reminds us that part of being a missional community means an ongoing commitment to expansion and reaching new seekers with the gospel. His correspondence with the Romans views his visit with Rome as a stepping-stone for his true goal of proclaiming the Messiah Jesus in Gaul (Spain). To read the New Testament accurately, we must recognize the ongoing apostolic mandate and steadfastly refuse to hear the biblical text as anything less than a guide for understanding, equipping, and unleashing God's people to engage our present world with the gospel.

## Paul's Missional Method

Paul's gospel centered on the death and resurrection of Jesus (1 Cor. 2:2). These were Paul's non-negotiables (1 Cor. 2:2; 15:3–5). Paul, however, adapts the language of the gospel to engage his audience within their culture. Paul does not preach to Jews and Greeks in the same way (1:18–25). Paul translates the gospel so that people can actually hear its good news clearly. Paul describes his method in 1 Corinthians 9:22: "I have become all things to all people so that by all possible means I might save some." Paul is not being deceptive; he is being incarnational. As Jesus took on human flesh to show us the fullness of God, Paul adapts his practices depending on his audience. To Jews (or Greeks attracted to Judaism), he generally teaches about Jesus from the Old Testament Scriptures (Acts 17:10–15). To Greeks, he uses language drawn from their culture (Acts 17:16–34).

Paul's approach places a high value on people. By using common language, Paul allows potential Christ-followers to hear the gospel unfettered by unfamiliar words or by Old Testament practices. Readers unfamiliar with the Old Testament are often surprised that Paul talks so much about circumcision in his letters in the New Testament. Circumcision was a Jewish marker of identity (see Gen. 17). Paul argues strongly that Greeks did not have to become Jews by receiving circumcision as the precondition for joining the Christ-following movement (e.g., Gal. 3:28; 5:1–12). Paul upholds the Old Testament law of love (Rom. 13:8–10), but removes dietary and ritual practices from it.

The gospel is for all people and Paul works tirelessly to announce the good news to the multitudes of his day. He desires to see transformed people from all cultures join God's kingdom and its mission. Paul writes, "For the kingdom of God is not a matter of eating and drinking, but of righteousness, peace and joy in the Holy Spirit" (Rom. 14:17). It is calling people back to their truest humanity for the sake of the world.

Paul began his life as a strict Pharisee (Phil. 3:4–6). A life-changing encounter with Jesus transformed him into a cross-cultural vessel of God's grace for all. This is God's desire for us, too. The gospel comes to us on its way to someone else. Let us follow Paul in his commitment to people and his unswerving confidence in Jesus' death and resurrection as the core of the gospel.

## Questions for Reflection

How would you tell a friend about the good news of Jesus using language that he or she would understand?

_____

_____


How would our community of faith need to change to embrace Paul's "go to" mission?

_____

_____

# DAY 4

# God's Future and the Present Mission of the Church

Read 2 Corinthians 4:1–5:10; 1 Thessalonians 4:13–5:11;
Revelation 1–3; 21:1–6

*But you, brothers and sisters, are not in darkness so that this day should surprise you like a thief. You are all children of the light and children of the day. We do not belong to the night or to the darkness. So then, let us not be like others, who are asleep, but let us be awake and sober. For those who sleep, sleep at night, and those who get drunk, get drunk at night. But since we belong to the day, let us be sober, putting on faith and love as a breastplate, and the hope of salvation as a helmet. For God did not appoint us to suffer wrath but to receive salvation through our Lord Jesus Christ. He died for us so that, whether we are awake or asleep, we may live together with him. Therefore encourage one another and build each other up, just as in fact you are doing.—1 Thessalonians 5:4–11*

---

**Core Truth:** The New Testament's vision of future abundance grounds the call to faithful living in a courageous confidence of God's final victory.

---

The New Testament writers recognize that God's victory through the life, death, and resurrection of Jesus secures the future. The pages of the New Testament are full of visions of God's future. God's future is bright and good. It is one of abundant love and mercy. It is the full reversal of the effects of human sin and brokenness. It includes the full redemption of all creation. It marks the return of peace and rest. It involves the climactic consummation of God's future kingdom.

## Inspiration for Today; Not Speculation for Tomorrow

Many students of the Bible focus their reading on trying to predict the end of the world. However, the Bible does not give a precise road map to the end. As humans, we may long to connect God's future to our calendar, but this is not the goal of the New Testament. The New Testament writers describe God's future for the purpose of inspiring a courageous faithfulness in believers. Since God's future is secure, God's people are able to live as his missional people in the present. The New Testament's vision grounds faithful living in a dogged and daring confidence in God's final victory.

## Jesus and the Future

Jesus' preaching about the kingdom is present–future oriented. Jesus' proclaimed "kingdom of heaven [God] has come near" (Matt. 4:17; cf. Mark 1:15). Jesus' disciples carried the same announcement (Matt. 10:7). The message of the kingdom announces the immediate arrival of God's age of salvation in Jesus the Messiah while anticipating a triumphant future.

The kingdom vision of the New Testament holds in tension the "already present" and "not yet fully consummated." In Jesus' longest block of teaching on the future (Matt. 24–25), he offers a series of stories to paint pictures of the end times. His words focus on remaining faithful by standing firm and avoiding being deceived. Moreover, disciples show themselves ready for the end through serving as good stewards of God's gifts. This especially includes practicing justice and mercy to the marginalized. Jesus' life and his resurrection demonstrate the fullness of God's future and inspired confidence in his followers to engage fully in God's mission to the world of making disciples (Matt. 28:16–20). The Great Commission ends with Jesus guaranteeing both his presence and their future: "And surely I am with you always, to the very end of the age" (v. 20).

## Paul and the Future

Paul looks forward with anticipation to the full redemption of all creation (Rom. 8:18). His writings encourage God's people to faithfulness in light of the hope that they have in the resurrection of Jesus. For Paul, this involves the future experience of resurrection of the body. Jesus' resurrection was the first fruit of the final resurrection that God will do to transform our fragile and broken bodies into the likeness of Jesus' resurrected body. It is life in a transformed body in the new age that is coming (1 Cor. 15; 2 Cor. 4:1–5:10).

In reading through Paul's letters, we will continually find images of the coming abundance of God's future. Paul wants his churches to be absolutely certain that the future is secure. Paul gives these words as a means of encouraging God's people. For example, in an extended section (1 Thess. 4:13–5:11), Paul encourages (4:18 and 5:11) God's people by assuring them of the security of loved ones who have died in the faith (4:13–18) and of the certainty of the future (5:1–11).

## Revelation and the Future

The book of Revelation is a call for holy living in the present. Revelation opens with a series of exhortations to faithfulness in letters to seven churches (Rev. 1–3). Each church has its own challenges in living out the gospel. Revelation serves the church by naming the dangers of living as God's people in an empire that does not recognize Jesus' lordship, immersed in an economic system that knows no compromise, surrounded by idols that lure the faithful away from their first love, and inundated by plurality of religious options at variance with the gospel. Yet Revelation envisions a vibrant witness regardless of circumstances. Revelation's call to holiness is rooted in the apocalyptic visions of Revelation 4–21. In essence, Revelation's message may be summarized thusly: *live holy lives as God's witnesses now because God has control of the future and Jesus, the Living Lord of the church, will return to usher in the New Creation.*

Revelation 22 draws the book to a conclusion with repeated promises of Jesus' return. "Look I am coming soon!" (22:7). "He who testifies to these things says, 'Yes, I am coming soon.' Amen. Come, Lord Jesus" (22:20). Christ-followers can be faithful in the present moment because God is faithful and his final victory has already been won through the Lord Jesus.

## Questions for Reflection

What is the purpose of the New Testament's announcement of God's future age of abundance?

_____

_____

What is the basis for your hope in a good future?

_____

_____

How would you live differently if you knew that your future was absolutely secure in God?

_____

_____

# DAY 5

# New Creation: The Fullness of Salvation

### Read Revelation 21:1–6

*Then I saw "a new heaven and a new earth," for the first heaven and the first earth had passed away, and there was no longer any sea. I saw the Holy City, the new Jerusalem, coming down out of heaven from God, prepared as a bride beautifully dressed for her husband. And I heard a loud voice from the throne saying, "Look! God's dwelling place is now among the people, and he will dwell with them. They will be his people, and God himself will be with them and be their God. He will wipe every tear from their eyes. There will be no more death or mourning or crying or pain, for the old order of things has passed away." He who was seated on the throne said, "I am making everything new!" Then he said, "Write this down, for these words are trustworthy and true." He said to me: "It is done. I am the Alpha and the Omega, the Beginning and the End. To the thirsty I will give water without cost from the spring of the water of life."—Revelation 21:1–6*

---

**Core Truth:** God's vision of New Creation serves to inspire God's people to embody and proclaim his kingdom to all in anticipation of his abundant future.

---

The biblical story reaches its climax in New Creation. Revelation 21:1–6 serves as a potent witness to the beauty, grandeur, and bliss of God's future New Creation.

The Bible ends in a similar way to its beginning. Creation and New Creation are the bookends of the biblical story. Without them, it is difficult to make sense of our lives in the world. The world we live in today is not as

God intended. We are now living in the age of God's redeeming work and we can live confidently because we know that God's future New Creation is coming.

## New Creation

### An Urban Future

In Genesis, humanity begins in a garden. But Revelation ends with the vision of a New Jerusalem rather than a new Eden. In the aftermath of the expulsion from Eden, Adam and Eve's son Cain founded the first city.

Cities are a mixed bag in the Scripture. We'll start with the negative. Cain's founding of a city comes in response to his sense of alienation and loneliness (Gen. 4:17). The building of the city of Babel with its tower epitomized human rebellious pride (Gen. 11:1–9).

Cities also could be centers of wickedness. Sodom and Gomorrah are notable examples (Gen. 18:16–19:29). At the imploring of Abraham, God rescues Lot and his family from the destruction of those cities. The book of Revelation envisions wickedness in the form of the city Babylon (Rev. 17–18). Its defeat is a victory for the mission of God. Babylon represents the human status quo post-fall and seeks to suppress the kingdom of God by suffocating all who oppose its all-encompassing moral–economic–political system. This reality is the ongoing challenge to God's people who seek to live holy and faithful lives in the midst of nations and people allied to a different kingdom.

However, in Deuteronomy, God promises his people cities to dwell in (6:10). Cities were also marked off as places of refuge (Deut. 19:1–13). The worship of the LORD centered in Jerusalem. Jerusalem (Zion) became the tangible expression of God's residence on earth:

> Great is the LORD, and most worthy of praise,
> in the city of our God, his holy mountain.
> Beautiful in its loftiness,
> the joy of the whole earth,
> like the heights of Zaphon is Mount Zion,
> the city of the Great King.
> God is in her citadels;
> he has shown himself to be her fortress. (Ps. 48:1–3)

In the book of Jonah, Nineveh is the target of Jonah's mission. Nineveh is a great and wicked city (1:1). However, the book emphasizes God's concern for the human and animal inhabitants of the city (4:11). God desires to transform even the wicked Ninevites through his love. God is concerned about Nineveh because God is for life and good. This balances the tales of Sodom, Gomorrah, and Babylon. God's intentions throughout the Scriptures have been to bring wholeness to his creation.

The Bible's urban vision is profound. In Revelation, humanity's final destination centers on a New Jerusalem on a New Earth. In 2008, the majority of the world's population had moved to urban areas for the first time in human history. In anticipation of the New Jerusalem, God's people need to embrace the urbanization of our world by establishing missional communities in the urban centers around our globe. This was Paul's primary method in the New Testament era. He carried the gospel to cities in the hope that urban centers would then impact the surrounding rural regions. God is waiting for his people today to catch this vision and engage our world's great populations centers with the good news of the kingdom.

## Relational Wholeness

In God's future, reconciliation is complete. There is a return to the Edenic reality of Genesis 1–2. New Jerusalem replaces Eden, but the central reality remains: the presence of the Creator God with his people. Harmony returns between God and humanity, men and women, and humanity and the rest of creations. Justice, love, and righteousness permeate all aspects of reality.

## True Security

The security of God's future trumps any danger and tenuousness in the present. This truth creates a foundation for every woman and man to be unleashed to live as the person whom God created them to be. The vision of God's ultimate victory emboldens us to recognize a loving and just world worthy of our lives.

Conversely, God's future is greater than the joys and happiness that we may find in the now. In our modern world of affluence and pleasure, we need to reflect on the future vision of the New Testament from a different angle. The New Testament's vision of God's final victory calls us to live for a greater vision than our own security and personal enjoyment. God's future beckons

Christ-followers to a way of love and justice worthy of our best. Or to put it another way: Jesus models a way worthy of our greatest gifts, talents, and passions—one worth our lives and our deaths.

As Christ-followers, we live in a dynamic tension in which we recognize by faith a secured future without knowing the exact details. We follow Jesus into the world on mission in anticipation of the New Creation. Yet we remember the words of Jesus, "But about that day or hour no one knows, not even the angels in heaven, nor the Son, but only the Father" (Matt. 24:36).

## Mission

God's mission to bring reconciliation and redemption to humanity and all creation moves forward under God's promise of a secure future. The New Testament church evangelized in the earnest expectation of Jesus' imminent return to usher in the kingdom. God's future is beautiful. God's future is secure. Therefore, the mission of God's people goes forward. In the New Testament era, Christians were a tiny minority. They faced hardships and persecution for their allegiance to Jesus as Lord over the Roman world's suffocating vision for humanity. Early Christians found themselves persecuted by both Gentiles and Jews. Thus, the choice to follow Jesus was costly. The New Testament's vision of New Creation, therefore, is profoundly concerned with grounding Jesus' followers with a courageous hope in God's final victory so that they may function as instruments and agents of God's reconciling gospel. Let us recapture this vision to empower our own witness.

## Questions for Reflection

How does the Bible's vision of New Creation bring the biblical story to a climax?

_____

_____

How is your community of faith seeking to advance Jesus' kingdom?

_____

_____

Who is your mission?

_____

_____

Who is your community that will take the journey of faith with you?

_____

_____

What kind of person do you need to become to live as part of God's missional community in/to/for the world?

_____

_____

# Church and New Creation

## CORE TRUTHS

1. The Holy Spirit empowers God's people to carry the good news of the gospel to all people.
2. Paul proclaims a gospel that reconciles humanity and all creation through the life, death, and resurrection of Jesus.
3. The gospel calls all of God's people to engage in acts of witness to the surrounding world.
4. The New Testament's vision of future abundance grounds the call to faithful living in a courageous confidence of God's final victory.
5. God's vision of New Creation serves to inspire God's people to embody and proclaim his kingdom to all in anticipation of his abundant future.

## OPEN SESSION WITH PRAYER

## DEBRIEF THE READING FOR THE WEEK (15 MINUTES)

- What were the key takeaways that you gained from this week's reading?
- What aspects of the reading did you find confusing?
- What role does the Holy Spirit serve in the advance of God's mission?
- What purpose do the New Testament visions of New Creation serve in the life of faith?
- How does the gospel bring reconciliation to humanity and all creation?

## WATCH VIDEO (30 MINUTES)

## CONVERSATION (15 MINUTES)

- What aspects of the message resonated with you most deeply?
- What questions did Brian's talk raise for you?
- How well do we embody the New Testament's vision of a missional community to go and makes disciples?
- How would you tell a friend about the good news of Jesus using language that he or she would understand?
- How would we live differently if we knew that our future was absolutely secure in God?
- Who is your mission?
- Who is your community that will take the journey of faith with you?
- What kind of person do you need to become to live as part of God's missional community in/to/for the world?

## CLOSING PRAYER

# Notes

1. Thomas Jackson, ed. *The Works of John Wesley* (Grand Rapids: Baker, 1979), 5:3.

2. *Aurelius Augustine*, translated by Edward Pusey, vol. VII, part 1, *The Harvard Classics* (New York: P. F. Collier & Son, 1909–14); Bartleby.com, 2001. www.bartleby.com/7/1/, Book Eight, chapter 12, paragraphs 27–28.

3. The book of Deuteronomy serves to retell the message of Sinai to the next generation of God's people and covers much of the same themes.

4. See parallel passage in Mark 1:14–15.

5. Dietrich Bonhoeffer, *Creation and Fall: A Theological Exposition of Genesis 1–3,* translated by Douglas Stephen Bax; ed. by John W. de Gruchy; Dietrich Bonhoeffer Works, 3; (Minneapolis: Fortress, 2004), 111.

6. Oswald Chambers, *My Utmost for His Highest: Features the Author's Daily Prayers* (Grand Rapids, MI: Discover House Publishers, 1994), 21.

7. For the sake of clarity, we have referred to Abram by his final name Abraham throughout this chapter. The book of Genesis uses Abram until God grants him the name Abraham (17:5).

8. http://www.independent.co.uk/news/world/nelson-mandela-10-inspirational-quotes-to-live-your-life-by-8988290.html?action=gallery&ino=3.

9. Private conversation with Dr. Robert Tuttle.